DOWN TO EARTH

Out-of-the-Box Worship for Advent, Christmas and Epiphany

ROSIE RUSHTON

kevin
mayhew

kevin
mayhew

First published in Great Britain in 2012 by Kevin Mayhew Ltd
Buxhall, Stowmarket, Suffolk IP14 3BW
Tel: +44 (0) 1449 737978 Fax: +44 (0) 1449 737834
E-mail: info@kevinmayhewltd.com

www.kevinmayhew.com

ISBN 978 1 84867 528 5
Catalogue No. 1501360

Cover design by Rob Mortonson
© Images used under licence from Shutterstock Inc.
Edited by Lawrence Osborn
Typeset by Richard Weaver

Printed and bound in Great Britain

Contents

About the author

Rosie Rushton is a Reader in the Diocese of Peterborough and the author of more than forty books for teenagers and young adults. In both roles she is passionate, not only about presenting the life-changing message of the Good News in ways that are relevant to our fast-changing, anxious and media-driven world, but also about exploring 'down-to-earth' ways of worshipping the Christ who came to this earth with a message of love, peace, encouragement and joy that has never been more relevant or more yearned-for than it is today.

Some of the material in these services has been adapted from *The Greatest Love Story Ever Told – And Then Some!*, Rosie's interpretation, through the eyes of four young people, of the three years of Jesus' earthly ministry.

Introduction

At this time of year, the advertising industry goes into overdrive, presenting us with images of the 'perfect' Christmas; smartly dressed parents with immaculately clean children, clustering round a Christmas tree or piling perfectly cooked turkey and vegetables onto their plates and never once uttering the words 'Yuk! What's that?' The subliminal message is that as long as we buy the right brand of trainers, the latest Wii game and the just-released, totally updated iPhone, our children will adore us, our friends will envy us and our social standing will go up a couple more notches. And we know it's false, and we laugh at people who are taken in by it and end up in debt as a result. We see ourselves as being the sensible ones, the ones who know the reality of economic downturn, advertising hype and the nine-day wonders of the manufacturing industry. We are the ones who see the reality behind the airbrushed images. No one pulls the wool over our eyes. We see it as it really is.

Or do we? When we send our Christmas cards, bearing images of an airbrushed Virgin and child with not a speck of dirt on them, do we pause and wonder whether Mary had the baby blues or whether Joseph was worried sick about leaving his carpentry business for longer than he'd planned? Do we consider Jesus with colic, or Mary, exhausted from lack of sleep? Or are we taken in by the hymn writers' ideas of the sweetly sleeping infant, 'little Lord Jesus, no crying he makes'? When we sing of angels visiting shepherds on a windswept hillside, do we pause to wonder whether those men were written off as delusional by their families and friends? And when we hear the story of the Magi and their costly gifts, and read about Mary and Joseph fleeing at a moment's notice to a strange country, do we take ourselves forward to that massacre of innocent children when the streets of Bethlehem echoed, not with the song of angels, but with the anguished cry of women whose babies were being torn from their arms?

The wonder, the miracle of Christmas is that God came down to earth to dwell among us, to live as one of us, to experience the things we experience without some heavenly analgesic to make the nasty bits less painful. His adult ministry lasted barely three years: he lived as a baby, a child, an adolescent and a young adult for thirty years.

Most of the people who knew him during those three decades never made it into the Bible stories, just as the vast majority of the people in the crowds that followed him during his ministry are never named or known. And yet the crowd who 'marvelled at these things' were changed forever by their encounter with the living God and maybe, just maybe, if we can break free from our stereotyped images, artistic presentations and habitual interpretations of this familiar and deeply loved story, we too can not only encounter Christ in a new way but be swamped by that overpowering sense of awe and wonder and gratitude that comes with realising that we too, as part of the crowd who follows him in the twenty-first century, are welcomed by him, warts and all, and that we need not be spotless and pure and holier than thou to feel the healing, gracious touch on our lives. For, like those who knew him two thousand years ago, we are invited to come to our Lord just as we are.

How to use the reflections

The reflections in this book can be used in a variety of ways: in place of a sermon or teaching slot, as the focus of the Ministry of the Word element of a Eucharistic service, or as stand-alone reflections to form part of an Advent course. Many of them lend themselves to adaptation into sketch or playlet form for use in youth groups and secondary school assemblies, and all have been written with a variety of worship spaces in mind – from churches and school halls to scout huts, open-air spaces and houses.

Many are offered within the format of a Service of the Word; but each element can be taken 'off the peg' when the full service is not required. I have purposely not recommended specific translations for the Scripture readings. However, I would humbly suggest that there are occasions on which using a translation with which a congregation is less familiar – for example, *The Message* – may shed new light and give pause for fresh reflection. Likewise, for those unused to the poetry of the King James Version, certain readings lend themselves to this translation.

Suggested prayers are included; those referred to as 'Prayers of intercession' have introductory prayer after which leaders are free to include those prayers most relevant to the needs of their congregation, community and the wider world at the time.

I have made suggestions for hymns, worship songs and other resources, but clearly those leading worship will have their own take on what works best for their congregation and facilities. But one thing is to be encouraged: *space for silence*! I have suggested points at which these silences might naturally fall, but these are only suggestions and worship leaders may feel that other places in the service are more appropriate. Wherever it comes, silence there must be for personal reflection and for the chance to hear the still, small voice of our ever-present God.

1

Waiting

A service for Advent Sunday

*The service should start in silence with Leader/Minister in place, choir if relevant in choir stalls – but no words should be spoken for **three** minutes after the advertised start time. There will probably be shuffling, coughing, whispering from the congregation, but those leading or participating in the service should remain still, silent and apparently unaware. After three minutes the Leader stands.*

Leader

Welcome! I am so pleased to have kept you waiting.

I guess that's not what you expected me to say. Tardiness is usually an occasion for an apology – but today sees the start of the season of Advent, and waiting is part of what Advent is all about. And it's not just about waiting for Christmas; not just about waiting to celebrate the birth of the infant Christ in a stable in Bethlehem. It's about waiting for and reflecting on the time when he will come again in power and glory.

For some, that may feel even more uncomfortable as sitting here for a few minutes in silence, wondering what on earth was going on; whether anything was going to happen, or whether this was going to be one of those silent services which, let's face it, can be something of a challenge, can't they? All that quiet with no words to fill the void, all that time to face our thoughts. So much easier just to get on with it – sing the songs, speak the liturgy – anything that will keep our minds occupied and our bodies busy. But all this talk of waiting for Christ to come again? That – although of course we wouldn't say it out loud – is pretty scary stuff. Much easier to keep Christ in the manger, tightly wrapped up and helpless; or somewhere ascended in the heavens, receiving our thoughts and prayers, as and when we have time, rather than imagine him returning now, here, breaking into our world and seeing us just as we are.

And yet to imagine that is one of the great joys and gifts of the Advent season. We may not know the time of his future coming, but Christ yearns to come again right now – he aches to be let in to our individual worlds, into the pain we struggle to hide, into the anger we are ashamed to acknowledge, into the emptiness we long to have filled.

Waiting is never easy: but whether we wait in hope and certain expectation, or with doubts and niggles and anxieties – Christ will come to us again, just as he did to others long ago.

Hymn

Open our eyes, Lord (we want to see Jesus)

Lighting of the Advent candle

(*During the lighting of the candle, the appropriate verse of the following carol is sung.*)

Carol

Christmas is coming

Readings

Isaiah 9:6
Luke 2:25, 26

Reflection of Simeon

You know, at times, I began to doubt my own sanity, to think I was delusional or suffering from the fantasies of old age. Mostly, it was on the bad days that I felt like that: days when every bone in my body ached, when my sight – never brilliant at the best of times – became so clouded and unreliable that I had to reach out and touch the pillars of the Temple to find my way around. I could feel the end of my life creeping up on me and still nothing – or rather no one.

Had I been imagining God's words to me? Had I been mistaken when I heard him tell me that before I died, I would see his promised Messiah with my own eyes? I had literally been waiting a lifetime for that promise to be fulfilled, and now it seemed that my weary body would give up on me and all the waiting would have been for nothing.

I knew he would come one day; it wasn't God I doubted, it was whether I was the one who would see him. Day after day the words of the prophet Isaiah would ring in my ears, words proclaiming the birth of a child who would be called Wonderful Counsellor, Mighty God, Everlasting Father and Prince of Peace. And like Isaiah, I found myself pleading, sobbing almost 'Oh that you would rend the heavens and come down! Come down to make your name known.'

And still I waited.

Hymn

Come, thou long-expected Jesus

Reading

Luke 2:27-32

Simeon

The Temple was crowded that day, even more crowded than usual. The noise was deafening, people bartering, priests chanting, sacrificial doves and lambs cooing and bleating. My eyes were smarting, partly from the weariness of another sleepless night due to the pain in my hips and knees, and partly from the smoke of the incense.

But then suddenly, they were clear. Clearer than they had been in months – and that's when I saw the young couple. They were climbing the 15 steps that lead up to the Gate of Nicanor and in that brief moment as my eyes took in the pretty young woman, gazing so proudly at her baby, and the rather anxious, travel-worn man beside her, I knew. I knew that this child they were bring to the Temple was the one. Don't get me wrong – there was nothing to mark this baby out from any of the other infants being brought for presentation at the

Temple. He was a cute little thing, but no different from a dozen other Jewish babies.

But still I knew.

The child's mother walked right up to me, and as she handed over her precious bundle for the ritual of the law to be carried out, her eyes met mine. In that moment, I saw it all; the love of God, the love of the child, the weight of responsibility and the knowledge, buried deep but always there, of the pain to come. And the reason I could see it had nothing to do with me; it was a gift of insight given to me by God – the God who was keeping his promise made years before.

And in that moment, the waiting and the wondering, the doubting and pain simply didn't matter any more.

My voice cracked as I blessed the child; the emotion was almost too much to bear. I remember words poured from my lips, almost without my thinking them first.

'God,' I said. 'You can let me, your servant, die now. Release me in peace as you promised. With my own eyes, I have seen your salvation: it is now out in the open for everyone to see. A God-revealing light to the non-Jewish nations, and of glory for your own people Israel.'

Hymn

I've waited long *or* Now Lord, according to thy word

Reading

Luke 2:33-35

Simeon

It was as the couple turned to leave that I knew my job wasn't finished. Not yet. I looked from one to the other and then, on a Spirit-driven impulse, took the young mother to one side. She looked up at me and I knew that the anxiety in her eyes would only deepen when she heard what I had to say.

I didn't know how to put it but the Holy Spirit urged me on.

'Mary,' I said. 'This child is chosen by God both to destroy and to save thousands of people in Israel. He will be a visible sign from God

– yet many will speak out against him and misunderstand him and by their behaviour, show themselves up for what they really are.'

I paused but God had not done with me.

'Sorrow, like a sharpened sword, will break your heart.'

Her face paled, and she briefly closed her eyes as if in pain. Then she raised her head and held my gaze. I laid my hand on her head, blessed her again, turned and left. My job was done. The waiting was over.

Hymn

Christ be our light *or* Hail to the Lord who comes

Prayer

Lord, Simeon must have held you, the infant Christ gently yet firmly, acknowledging your human frailty while worshipping your eternal divinity. Help us, so to hold you in our hearts that we offer you firm faith, patient trust and a never-ending willingness to wait for your purpose for our lives to be revealed in your own time. Amen.

Taizé chant

Wait for the Lord, whose day is near (*to be sung five times*)

Prayer

Lord, Simeon waited for long years before seeing the fulfilment of your promise. We too wait Lord: wait for the time when swords will be beaten into ploughshares and spears into pruning hooks, when nation will not take up sword against nation, and there will be war no more. We wait for the time when you will come and make all things new; we wait for the time when the earth will be filled with the glory of God as the waters cover the sea. But we know, Lord, that you do not call us to wait passively; may we be active in your service, lively in our response to the needs of others, proactive as we work for change, filled with praise as we see glimpses of the work of your hands in our world. Amen.

(*A time of silent prayer.*)

Leader

Simeon waited in hope and in expectation, in trust and with a stead-fast faith that God's word would be fulfilled. But not everyone who waits has hope, or expectation, or a faith that underpins and strengthens them in times of difficulty. For them, the waiting is even harder.

Reading

John 5:1-6

Reflection of the lame man

'Do you want to get well?' That's what he asked me – bold as you like! What sort of a stupid question was that? Did he think I was lying by the side of that pool just for the fun of it? OK, so I had a good spot in one of the alcoves: out of the sun in the summer, and sheltered from the wind in the winter – and of course, plenty of people passed by and tossed the odd coin my way. Sometimes people exchanged a word with me – abusive frequently but occasionally pitying. Some even gave me food. But no one had ever asked me such a daft question as he did.

'Do you want to get well?' Why else would I be waiting there, waiting for the waters of the pool to bubble up like they did from time to time? I knew the legend as well as anyone – the first person into the moving waters would be cured. The thing was, it wasn't a regular occurrence – you could wait for weeks and nothing happened, then there would be movement three times in one day.

There was no telling. No chance to plan. Not that planning would have made any difference for me.

You see, the moment there was the slightest movement on the surface of the pool, everyone hurried to jump in. It was all so unfair.

You can see that, can't you? It was the ones who *could* hurry, the people who didn't have much wrong with them, the ones who could move without help, or the ones who had a load of friends to pick them up and dump them in the water – they were the ones who got healed. (Or at least, I guess they did. They're in and out so fast and off about their business that you never really know if what was wrong with them has gone away or not.)

But me – I've never been lucky. No friends to speak of and no family left. I was just stuck there, day in day out, for years on end, my legs withered and useless. By the time I'd managed to shuffle a few inches, the pool was full, the water had stilled and that was that till the next time. Not my fault – just my bad luck, and to be honest, I'd long since given up even hoping for things to change. I guess I was just lying there waiting to die.

And then one day, this man comes – a rabbi, with a cluster of his followers tagging along behind. Now I see a lot of rabbis – it was a temple, after all – but aside from the odd glance or nod, none had ever taken very much notice of me.

But this man, this Jesus as I found out later he was called, came and stood right over me gazing down at me with this kind of puzzled expression on his face.

'Do you want to get well?'

I started to explain all about how I couldn't get into the water in time, how others always beat me to it, but he just waved my protests away.

'Get up, roll up your mat and start walking!' he said.

I could hear a few titters all around me – I even heard someone mutter, 'As if!' I backed off, shuffling on my bottom, edging away from him. I thought he was crazy – some kind of con artist. I thought that – until I looked up into his eyes. It was as if he could see right into my very soul – could see what I was thinking – see the doubts and the unspoken swear words and the anger at having him turn everyone's attention on to me.

But then he smiled. And slowly he nodded, held out his hand as if gesturing to the clear space ahead of me. That's when my legs began to tingle, and sensations like I hadn't felt in years made my feet burn and twitch.

'Get up! Pick up your mat and walk!'

Whether he actually said those words again, or whether they were just resonating in my head, I'm not sure but somehow I found myself on my knees and then I was levering myself up into a crouching position.

And then I stood. I put one foot in front of the other, and then again, and again. I was walking! I felt giddy – from an upright position, the ground seemed so far away.

I turned back to speak to him but he'd already moved on. I had to catch him, I had to thank him. I stooped down, grabbed my tattered mat and stumbled towards him.

Hymn

For the joys and for the sorrows (*For this I have Jesus*) *or* O for a thousand tongues to sing

Reading

John 5:10-13

Lame man

I really wanted to speak to him but they got in my way. A group of up-themselves Pharisees, swaggering and sneering – nothing new there then. But then one of them grabbed my arm and gestured to my mat.

'What do you think you're doing, carrying that on the Sabbath? Don't you know that working on the Sabbath is forbidden?'

You could hardly call it work, carrying a threadbare mat a few yards, but they looked pretty angry and no way was I about to take the blame. So I told them that the man who healed me told me to pick it up and walk; I told them that for the first time in 38 years I was mobile. All those years of waiting for the magic of the waters to work, and he does it in 10 seconds flat. I waited for the penny to drop. I waited for them to be amazed.

And you know what? The only thing they seemed interested in was finding the guy who had apparently encouraged me to break the rules. I couldn't believe it – worrying more over a stupid mat than over my new life. They kept asking who the man was and when I said

I didn't know his name they got a bit nasty, so I legged it. Yes, me – Old Shuffle Bottom! I actually ran into the Temple.

It seemed only right. I couldn't thank the man so I thought I ought to thank God.

Hymn

All for Jesus

Lame man

He found me there. Before I could speak a word he said 'Stop sinning!' I wanted to put him straight – tell him that I hadn't sinned. Well, how could I? When you can't move you can't do bad things that you see others do – you can't pick pockets or steal from market stalls. But even as I opened my mouth to protest, the words froze on my tongue. I had sinned. Over and over again. All those years of waiting had been filled with sin – the sin of jealousy of those who could walk, the sin of lust as I watched women walk by, the sin of hatred of my father who had cast me out rather than have to cope with a crippled son. I had envied those who had reached the pool in time, I had pretended to have no coins to spare when a kid even more deformed than me begged for a lepton to buy a piece of bread.

I felt tears well up in my eyes.

'Sin no more,' Jesus said.

And I didn't. I went to the Jews and pointed out the man Jesus to them. I assumed they all had relatives that needed healing. I didn't hang around after that but as I walked away I heard one of them say 'Wait. Wait till the moment is right.'

At the time, I just thought they meant they wanted to catch him when he was in a really good mood. But now, I wish I had kept my mouth shut.

Prayers of intercession

Lord, we want to be well. We want to be healed of all that displeases you, all that stains our life, everything that cripples us, slows us down and makes us unfit for purpose. For our purpose, Lord, is to serve you and one another and so often it is our prejudice, our laziness, our desire for an easy time, that prevents us from responding to your will. And yet, Father, at other times, we try so hard – we push ourselves too hard, we set ourselves goals and kid ourselves that it is you who wants us to work till we drop, take on so many responsibilities that we crumple under the load. May we always, Father, make space in our day to check in with you; to listen to your priorities which so often differ from our own – and then Father, we pray, give us the wisdom and the willingness to go about life your way and not our own. We pray it in Jesus' name. Amen.

(*Here follow intercessory prayers for the congregation, community and wider world.*)

Hymn

Thy kingdom come – on bended knee

Blessing and dismissal

2
Blessing and honour – the story of Zechariah

A service for Advent

Introduction

For years, Zechariah and Elizabeth had longed for a child. They had prayed in faith, lived month after month, year after year, in hope – and their prayers had gone unanswered. And then, when they had resigned themselves to being childless, the unimaginable happened.

Wonderful, awe-inspiring – but why? Why did God take so long? Why did Elizabeth have to spend a lifetime overshadowed by the perceived shame of barrenness? Why wait until age would make it harder to give birth, harder to rear a lively child? Why did God let that happen to the wife of one of his own faithful, devoted priests?

We don't know, and it doesn't matter that we don't. What matters is that in this season of Advent, when we can be almost overwhelmed with the hugeness of the themes of salvation and the coming kingdom, we look afresh at Zechariah and Elizabeth and we see two faithful people who had perhaps grown resigned to their dream of parenthood not being fulfilled. Their expectations were that it was all too late. Perhaps we too have elements of our lives that seem to be beyond rescuing, beyond changing. Advent is a time for considering the big themes, yes; but it is most of all a time for rekindling hope, for taking a long, hard look at our relationship with God, at the solidness of our faith and of our trust in the Lord. God promises that the best is yet to come. And it will be worth the wait.

Opening prayer

Gracious God, as we prepare to worship you, open our hearts and minds that we may respond to you. Still the urgency of our prayers of self-seeking and replace them with the stillness of mind and spirit that wait patiently to hear and understand your purpose. Lord, we struggle to wait; we find it so much easier to tell you what we want. But Lord, our deepest yearning is to know you, to serve you and to do your will. Help us, gracious God, when we stumble or tire and forgive us our times of doubting and disbelief. We ask it in Jesus' name. Amen.

Hymn

O worship the King

Reading

Luke 1:5-25

Reflection of Zechariah

(*Note: The character of Zechariah will be seated, and silent, with only physical gestures and facial expressions to denote memories and mood. The reader, if at all possible, should be hidden from the sight of the congregation and the following words will be read as a voiceover, since Zechariah has been struck dumb.*)

That day in the Temple at Jerusalem . . . oh, how I wish I had not doubted! Had I not questioned God's purpose, his plan . . . well, I would still be able to speak. Instead here I am, unable to carry out my priestly duties and constantly having to use sign language to make myself understood. Elizabeth is so patient; but I can see she longs to have a two-way conversation once again! At least Mary can give her that.

I feel so ashamed. I had longed and prayed for the day when I, Zechariah, priest of the Abija division of the Temple service corps, would be chosen by the drawing of lots to enter the inner sanctuary, the Holy of Holies, to burn the incense. When it came, I felt so joyful, so honoured to be the one to serve God in this way.

And then I messed it all up.

I had travelled from my home to the Temple in Jerusalem. An uneventful journey and yet on the way as I heard my companions speak of their families, their children, and in one case, a grandchild born just the day before – well, I remember wondering whether God was punishing us by ignoring all the years of prayer and devotion and sacrifice. But once I got to Jerusalem, and the day for the ceremony dawned, I put my grief behind me, conscious only of the honour that lay ahead, and the joy that would come from God in his Temple.

Hymn

O worship the Lord in the beauty of holiness

Zechariah

I had taken the incense into the inner sanctuary; outside the people were praying. Listening to the familiar chanting I felt an overwhelming sense of the presence of God; I prepared to light the taper and that was when I saw him, standing at the right-hand side of the altar, gazing straight at me, iridescent, fluid, yet recognisable. An angel.

I remember crying out, dropping the taper which brushed against my bare left foot. I have the mark to this day. And then the angel spoke.

'Do not be afraid, Zechariah. God has heard your prayer.'

My heart was pounding so loudly in my chest I could hardly hear his words.

That's when he told me that Elizabeth would soon be pregnant and we would have a son.

I remember thinking that either he or I was mad – and since angels come from God and are above such things, it must be me. For one thing, Elizabeth was barren and now her monthly cycle had all but stopped – the whole idea was ludicrous, an impossibility.

'And you must call him John,' the angel went on.

Well, obviously I was hallucinating – because a firstborn son would be named after me – or if not for me, at least for my father or grand-father. There were no Johns in my lineage.

Again I opened my mouth to speak, but the angel hadn't finished.

'This child will bring you joy like you have never known before, joy that everyone will share because they will sense and know that he is one of God's special, chosen men.'

At that, my pounding heart actually missed a beat. All my life I had prayed that I could do something, anything, special for God and now it seemed as if that prayer was being answered.

The angel's face was radiant; he said that from the moment of the child's conception he would be filled with God's Holy Spirit, that he would grow up to do amazing work for God and be the kind of man who would get God's message across to people who had never really got it before.

His words should have filled me with awe and wonder and for just a second my heart was filled with hope. But then my head took over.

'Stop!' I cried.

Even now I can hear the impatience and irritation in my voice and the shame and regret at what I said next will be with me till the day I die.

'It doesn't make sense,' I cried. 'How can that possibly happen? I'm old, my wife is past childbearing age – what you are talking about is impossible!'

In that instant, the radiance on the angel's face clouded. The timbre of his voice changed and the exhalation of his breath turned the air around me suddenly cold.

'I am Gabriel,' he said. 'I come from God to give you this message. But you won't believe me. And so, from now until your son is born you won't be able to utter a single word. You will be struck totally dumb.'

I opened my mouth to plead forgiveness, but I could not make a sound. Not even a guttural groan in my throat. Nothing.

'Everything I have said will happen,' said the angel. 'It will happen in God's time and because he has chosen to make it happen.'

And then suddenly the sanctuary was empty and I was alone. And totally, frighteningly dumb.

Silence

Prayer

God our Father, it is sometimes so hard to get our heads around your power, your purposes for us and your way of entering our lives in the most unexpected fashion. So often we want to believe but struggle with the enormity and mystery of your interaction with us. Forgive us, Lord, when we doubt and question; take our uncertainties and through the guidance of your Holy Spirit, lead us to a place of calm acceptance and vibrant eagerness to do your will, however challenging or unexpected that may be. We pray it in Jesus' name. Amen.

Hymn

Breathe on me, breath of God *or* Come down, O Love divine

Reflection of Elizabeth

(It is important that Elizabeth is played by a mature woman.)

He was weeping when he came home. My Zechariah – strong, faithful and committed – sobbed like a baby as he scratched word after word on the wax tablet, telling me what had happened at the Temple. With every word I read, the most extraordinary peace flooded my body – it was as if every muscle, every fibre of my being softened and relaxed.

I held him in my arms until he was quiet. Then I led him to our sleeping place and lay down with him. For I knew that every word the angel had said was going to come true. But I knew that maybe this time, even the Lord God himself would need a little help from us.

Within a week I knew I was with child.

Taizé chant

Laudate Dominum

Reflection of Elizabeth's servant girl

To be honest, when the mistress told me, I thought she had lost her marbles. I mean, it was ridiculous – a woman of her age imagining she was pregnant! Everyone knew she was barren – the gossip at the well was that she must have done something bad for God to refuse to give her a child. Well, I knew the mistress and I knew she didn't have a bad bone in her body, but it wasn't my place to say anything so I just kept my head down.

But then one morning I found her retching over a basin. I panicked – was it the meal I had prepared the day before? Zechariah, the master, often told me I had my head in the clouds and that I should learn to concentrate more; he would be furious if I'd poisoned his beloved wife. He could be very stern, and I wasn't keen to be on the end of his sharp tongue. Not that being shouted at was a problem at the time – for weeks, he'd had something wrong with his throat; he didn't speak at all and kept himself to himself. I wasn't even allowed to serve him; the mistress was the only one to go near him.

I guess Elizabeth saw the worried look on my face as she wiped her mouth and sat down heavily on the stool. That's when she told me.

'I'm going to have a baby,' she said. 'But you must not tell a soul.'

Well, of course, I thought at once that she was going crazy. I've seen it before in old people. Their minds get all back to front and they're like little kids, back in a land of make-believe. But she just fixed me with those soft grey eyes of hers.

'The Lord has done this for me,' she said. 'He has shown favour to me and now I won't be the object of shame and pity any more.'

What could I say? You don't argue with the person who puts a roof over your head and feeds you a good meal every day. So I smiled and nodded and began planning how I would comfort her when she came back to her senses and realised that she had been imagining the impossible.

On YouTube link

'Nothing Is Impossible', video created by Celio Abbati (http://www.youtube.com/watch?v=0_lUYOlMKkw).

(This rendition of 'Nothing is impossible with God' is a lively, theatrical one – suitable for youth groups to interpret with song and worship band instead of the video.)

Servant girl

At first I thought she kept herself hidden away because deep down she knew all this talk of being pregnant was just a fantasy. But as the weeks went by and the morning sickness stopped, her stomach grew larger and her breasts swelled. And I knew that I had been wrong.

Against all the odds, against all logic, Elizabeth really was going to have a baby.

Zechariah was still dumb – not a word, not a sound passed his lips. The funny thing was, Elizabeth didn't seem worried. When I suggested that he should seek help from a physician, she just smiled. God, she said, had it all in hand.

Women do tend to go funny as they get older.

Hymn

Dear Lord and Father of mankind

Reading

Luke 1:57

Reflection of Zechariah

(The reader should still be hidden from the congregation.)

From the moment our beautiful son John was born I waited. Prayed incessantly and waited, expecting that any moment my voice would come back and I would be able to express in words my pride and joy in my dear wife and new baby. The angel had promised that when the child was born I would speak again, but day after day I remained mute. I prayed and prayed for God's forgiveness, wracked with guilt for questioning his purposes. And I know Elizabeth prayed too – with Mary gone, she missed the joys of conversation; I saw her lips working as we knelt together and through my half-closed eyes saw her glancing at me and then lifting her eyes to heaven.

And still we waited.

Silence

25

Hymn

I will wait upon the Lord

Zechariah

It was the day of John's circumcision and naming. And still I had no voice. I confess that I was angry; this was the day when a father stands up and announces the name of his firstborn son. So when one of the guests asked Elizabeth what the child was to be called, she was the one to reply.

'John.'

Well, you should have heard the response. Someone said that was a ridiculous name, another pointed out that there was no one called John in my ancestry and that the child should be named after me, or my father or my father's father. Then one of the old women glanced up at me and said:

'Zechariah would never allow that.'

She spoke as if I wasn't there. I snatched up my wax tablet and began writing. Then I raised the tablet up for everyone to see.

(*At this point, the reader remains silent, and the person playing Zechariah stands, raises his wax tablet and speaks out loud:*)

'His name is John.'

(*From this point on, Zechariah speaks and the voiceover fades.*)

My voice echoed round the room. I could speak.

For a moment no one spoke and then the room was filled with the babble of excited voices declaring that they had witnessed a miracle and that I sounded just as I always had. Elizabeth leapt to her feet and hugged me.

'As the angel promised,' she whispered. 'May God be praised.'

The emotion was too much for me. I took the baby from her arms and walked outside. I needed time and space, time and space to be with my God.

Reading

Luke 1:68-79 (*read by Zechariah*)

or a choral and congregational setting of the Benedictus may be sung here.

Prayers of intercession

Ever-present God, help us to find our voices – voices to proclaim your love to those for whom the word has little meaning; voices to speak out for those who cannot speak for themselves; voices to share the story of your Son's redeeming love freely given for us all. And when we speak, Lord, of your power in our lives, let us not be hypocritical; help us to speak of the challenges and the struggles, as well as the joys and the triumphs, so that others who are in dark and difficult places may know that your Light is always there, leading them on to the place and the purpose you have set aside uniquely for them. Amen.

(*Here follow intercessory prayers for the congregation, community and wider world.*)

Hymn

Blessed be the name of the Lord *or* Blessing and honour (*Ancient of days*)

Blessing and dismissal

3

On Jordan's bank

A service for Advent

The reflections should be read by different voices, if possible from different areas of the worship space. This service lends itself to dramatisation for narrator and actors for school assemblies or youth-led worship as well as within the traditional church environment.

Introduction

The story of John the Baptist may seem to us like a tale from a dim and distant past, when God spoke to prophets and everyone knew the Scriptures as well as we know our own email address. But the crowds that gathered by the River Jordan had yearnings and issues little different from those people around the globe today: a craving for peace and justice, a desire to the see an end to bigotry and tyrannical regimes and a longing for the age-old promise of a Saviour to be fulfilled. Some had high opinions of themselves; others had been dealt the kinds of blows that rid a person of even a vestige of self-esteem. They shared one thing in common, although doubtless few realised it at the time.

They witnessed the start of something very, very big.

Prayer

Creator God, you made us to have imaginations, the ability to conjure up images in our minds, to explore places unvisited and things unseen. Help us now, we pray, to discern your Word for us as we journey back in word, prayer and meditation to the time when your Word as flesh was made known to those who had waited so long. Amen.

Hymn

On Jordan's bank the Baptist's cry *or* Comfort, comfort now thy people

Reading

Matthew 3:1-3

Reflection of a young bystander on the banks of the Jordan

It was hot, hotter than it should have been for the time of year. Not a breath of air stirred the surface of the water and the leaves on the few acacia trees were motionless. There was a sort of heaviness in the air that precedes a violent storm; but as yet there were no dark clouds looking and even if there had been, I doubt any of us would have noticed. Not while he was talking.

'Repent, for the kingdom of heaven is near!' His voice bounced off the limestone crags and reverberated around the crowd. 'Turn to God – the Lord is coming!'

I'd heard about John – well, everyone had. He wasn't exactly the kind of person to keep a low profile. He was wild looking, with hair that stood out in great matted tufts round his gaunt face and eyebrows that were grey with the dust of the desert edge. His tunic was made of rough hair and to be honest, it was filthy; but when he opened his mouth, all that faded away and there was just his voice, urgent and compelling. Even the few Roman soldiers who were ambling up and down through the crowd, giving the odd prod to a foot here, an elbow there, would occasionally stop dead in their tracks and turn, mesmerised by the thundering tones and sheer energy of the man.

'Come and be baptised, wash away your sins and be forgiven!'

Yeah, right. If only, I thought, it was that simple. A quick dip in the river and everything would be as new. Like that was ever going to happen. A lot of people said (although not to my face) that I was the way I was because of some sin my parents had committed. Well, they weren't around any more to get forgiven so could I just walk into the Jordan, ask for baptism and come out – come out like what? Looking normal and not twisted and deformed? Hardly. Able to speak so people understood me? Unlikely. And yet, what was there to lose? If it worked and life changed, great; if it didn't, at least I'd be cool for a few minutes. But I didn't make it to the water's edge, because just then some Pharisees turned up.

Reading

John 1:19-28

Reflection of a Pharisee

This man John had been on our minds for some time. As Pharisees, responsible for upholding the law and ensuring that the people know just what is required of them by God, we need to be one step ahead all the time, ready to quash false teachings, and to deal with people who spread messages that are not in line with the letter of the age-old law. To begin with, I was of a mind to let things be – there have been false prophets for years and the novelty soon wears off when the people realise that they are all fakes. But this John – well, he was different. It wasn't so much the baptising that bothered us: after all, any new convert to Judaism has to be fully immersed in water to be cleansed and ready for a new start in life. No, it was his growing influence with the people that had us worried. Every day, the rumours increased – people were saying that he was Elijah or perhaps Isaiah and, of course, claims like that couldn't go unchallenged.

And when we heard that people were speculating that John was the Christ we had been expecting for so long, we knew we couldn't wait a moment longer.

I was chosen to be one of the group sent to question John. When we got there, we found a cluster of priests and Levites standing close by, watching what was going on. John was standing on a rock a few feet out in the Jordan and I have to say, he looked every inch the prophet. Ragged, dressed in animal skins and with a voice resonating with passion and conviction. You could see how ignorant uneducated folk might be taken in by him.

He saw us coming and for a moment, as I saw him jump off the rock and into the water, I thought he was going to beat a hasty retreat. I couldn't have been more wrong. He strode right up to us, eyeballing Nicodemus who was leading the group and demanding to know whether we had come to be baptised.

I ask you – what kind of damn fool question was that? I could feel my blood beginning to boil and I kicked the mule forward and leaned over its shoulder so that I was so close to John I could feel his rancid breath on my face.

And I told him straight.

'We have no need of baptism – we are the descendants of Abraham. We are the favoured, chosen people of God.'

The crowd had grown quiet and for just a moment, I felt a sense of pride that I had been the one to silence this upstart. That was before he began ranting and raving at us, calling us a brood of vipers, saying that we needed to repent or be cast into the fire. Can you imagine how anyone could have the nerve to speak to us like that? We who live by the letter of the law every day of our lives, who teach others the way to be? For a moment I was rendered speechless by the man's arrogance, but one of the Levites walked up to him and asked outright whether he was Elijah. To his credit, he admitted at once that he wasn't – and added that he wasn't the anticipated Messiah either.

The question had to be asked.

'So just who do you think you are?'

Readings

(*two separate male voices*) John 1:23b; Matthew 3:11, 12

Pharisee

A strange sense of foreboding mixed with disbelief swept over me. He was claiming to be the fulfilment of the prophecy – saying that someone else was coming; no, was already among us; someone John said would be far greater than him. If this was true, then was he actually saying the true Messiah was coming soon, in our lifetime? Or was he just one more delusional fantasist?

Silence

Prayer

Lord God, we can be so very quick to condemn the Pharisees for not getting it. We seem to think they should have known that John the Baptist was sent by you, and no way a delusional fantasist, a man to be silenced and put down. And yet Lord, we know we are just as judgmental, just as quick to jump to conclusions – and just as confused in our choices of who to believe and who to follow. We are quick to succumb to advertising, to false images, to quick fixes; we often shy away from those who speak out forcefully about you – we prefer our sermons to be conciliatory and our evangelists to take the softly-softly approach. In John the Baptist you show us, Lord, that speaking your truth is never easy and challenging those who seek to destroy it is the work of each one of us, however hard that sounds. We are not all called to be orators or preachers; but we are all called to speak openly about what you have done and are doing in our lives. Help us, Lord, as we face this challenge every day. Amen.

Taizé chant

Wait for the Lord, his day is near

Reflection of John

You know, when I look back at that day, it's not the detail I remember. It's the emotion. First the deep frustration, the desperation to get the message across to those who I knew had come solely to nullify and disprove everything I was saying. I didn't care for myself – after all I was just the messenger. But I had this deep sense of time running out; of the fulfilment of what I knew I was on this earth to make clear drawing ever nearer and the very real fear that I was failing to get those who thought they knew it all to change their ways before it was too late. Some of them really seemed to want to get it: they called out their questions, asking what they should do to avoid being thrown into the fire. And I told them straight.

(*The person playing John reads Luke 3:11-14. It is suggested that* The Message *translation is used.*)

Of course, they didn't want to hear that, did they? The leader of the Pharisees turned his mule round and faced the crowd. He shouted to them that I was a troublemaker and that anyone paying attention to me would be going against all the law and the prophets. And with that, they rode off, kicking up clouds of dust into the faces of those standing nearby.

And it was at that moment, as they disappeared over the hilltop, that I saw him.

Hymn

Hark, a thrilling voice is sounding

Reading

Matthew 3:13-17

Reflection of the bystander

I have never seen a man change so fast. One minute, John was ranting and raving and shouting the odds at the Pharisees, and the next, his arms had dropped to his side and he was staring, open-mouthed, over the heads of the crowds to the path beyond.

I turned and saw at once who it was that he was watching. The man didn't look any different from a dozen others in the crowd – same dark curly hair, bushy black eyebrows and the beginnings of a growth of beard on his chin – but it was the way he moved that marked him out. He walked with long slow strides, his head nodding in rhythm with his steps as if he were mentally reassuring himself of where he was going. Despite the crowd pressing round him, occasionally brushing his arm, he just kept moving forward, not looking to left or right, his eyes fixed on John's face. It was as if he was oblivious to everything and everyone except the dishevelled guy standing in the water.

And as he drew nearer to the water's edge, John dropped to his knees and I could swear he was trembling.

I edged closer – up until now I could have stood half a furlong away and still heard every word John spoke but now he was barely whispering. The newcomer stopped at the water's edge and smiled at him.

'Is it – you? Jesus? I mean, you are the One?'

The man's voice was steady and gentle.

'Baptise me, John,' he said. And you know what? John shook his head. All this time he'd been pleading with people to get baptised and now someone begs for it, and he was refusing? It didn't make any sense.

'No, you should be baptising me, not the other way round,' John argued.

Jesus laid a hand on his shoulder.

'Just do it, John,' he said. 'This is the moment when God's work moves forward into a new place.'

I didn't have a clue what that meant but it seemed to satisfy John. He led Jesus deeper into the river and plunged him under the water.

Hymn

Lord, when you came to Jordan

Reflection of John

We looked at one another without speaking. There was no need for words. We had both heard it. The voice of God from heaven declaring, 'This is my beloved Son who delights me!' I had seen with my own eyes the pure white dove hovering over Jesus' head – the Spirit of God who had hovered over the waters of creation now creating something new, something beyond understanding and yet something that in the very depths of my being I knew to be right and true and just.

In that moment, I felt that everything would come right, that my life's purpose would be to watch and obey and follow the Messiah.

Not for one moment did I believe that I would end up here, in the stench and filth of a prison dungeon, forgotten it seems, even by the one whose coming I proclaimed.

This wasn't the way I expected things to turn out.

Prayer

God our Father, John the Baptist knew just who he was and who he wasn't. He understood your purpose for him and, in knowing that, had the courage to stand up to those who sought to put him down. Help us to know what it is that you are calling us to do for you – give us the obedience to embrace our calling and the courage to face any hardships or challenges it may bring. May we always recognise that our achievements come through your grace, and may we always give thanks that our shortcomings are forgiven through the love and sacrifice of your most precious Son. Amen.

Hymn

Hail to the Lord's anointed *or* Make way, make way

Blessing and dismissal

4

From rebirth to redeemed –
the story of Nicodemus

A service for Advent

Introduction

How do we see ourselves as we gather here today? As good Christian folk, secure in the knowledge that, as people of faith, we have sussed how to live, analysed and accepted the Word of Scripture and understood just what the Lord expects of us? Oh, I do so very much hope not. Because, wonderful as all that may sound, there is a very real danger in thinking of ourselves that way. Security and certainty can so often morph into complacency and arrogance. This service focuses on one man – a man of standing, an educated man, a man respected by his peers and committed to his faith – a man who despite the security of his life was drawn, despite himself, to explore and finally to embrace, a new Truth and a new Way. But the journey was not, as it never can be, without its pain.

Hymn

And can it be *or* Jesus calls us

Reading

John 3:1-17

Reflection of Nicodemus

I suppose the bottom line is that I was hedging my bets, sitting on the fence, keeping all my options open. The world I moved in was one where it was best to keep your own counsel, not let the other guys know what you were thinking. People thought that just because we were scholars, highly respected Jewish teachers and members of the

Sanhedrin, we were above all the petty politics and one-upmanship that lesser mortals engaged in.

Nothing could have been further from the truth.

Which is why I wasn't about to risk my credibility by starting a question and answer session with Jesus in broad daylight in the middle of the Temple forecourt. The fact was, I couldn't get the man out of my head; there was something about the way he spoke, the way he taught, that was so different, so fresh – and so challenging. There was something – well, godly about him. But I knew what my colleagues thought about him; and what they would think of me if they knew I wanted to find out more.

So I went at night. Well, late evening to be precise. I thought we could have a relaxed, informed discussion – I'm known for my debating skills, for the way I can draw people into revealing more than they really want to.

But I was in for the greatest shock of my life.

I thought I was getting off on the right foot. I told him that we all knew that he was a teacher sent from God because the miracles he performed couldn't happen without God's hand being in it. He just stared deep into my eyes and said,

'I tell you the truth, unless you are born again, you cannot see the kingdom of God.'

Well, I thought he was crazy and I almost said so. After all, I'm a high-born Jew – and high-born Jews are destined to get to heaven when their time comes. Or so I thought then. But I tried to stay calm and I asked him what on earth he meant: after all, once you've been born, you can hardly pop back into your mother's womb, can you?

I remember he smiled gently and shook his head. Then he said that a human mother gives birth to a flesh and blood baby that you can touch and see and cuddle; but inside, the essence of the person is formed by something you can't see – the Spirit. He said we have to be born from above, as well as from our mother's womb.

By then my head was buzzing, I can tell you and I was about to ask what this Spirit actually was, but he seemed to guess my confusion and explained before I had time to ask the question.

He said the Spirit was like the wind – you hear it, you see it rustling the leaves on the trees or whipping up waves on the lake but you have no idea where it comes from. And that's when things got a bit edgy.

I couldn't get my head around it all and I said so. And Jesus got quite irritated with me. I wasn't used to that – people in my position are used to being respected, honoured, grovelled to even, but it was quite a new experience to be asked how I could call myself a teacher when I didn't understand what he was telling me. Of course now, years down the line, I realise that I had so much to learn but back then – well, I was niggled, I admit it.

So while he was talking about Moses and about the Son of Man coming down from heaven, I was trying to get my anger under control. That was when he said something that I have never forgotten, something that, now I look back on it, changed the course of my life forever. He said:

'For God so loved the world that he gave his one and only Son that whoever believes in him shall not perish but have eternal life.'

Suddenly, I had an image in my head, an image of my son Seth as a newborn infant. One day he was staring around with that unfocused, newborn look and just a few weeks later, his eyes focused and he had that wide-eyed look of amazement that comes when you see things properly for the first time.

My meeting with Jesus in the dark and stillness of that night was the beginning of a new focus for my life. But I still had a very long way to go.

Hymn

God beyond knowledge *or* Teach me to dance

Reading

John 7:45-51

The son of Nicodemus reflects

I remember it so clearly. I'm grown up now of course, but back then I was just an 11-year-old boy, itching for the time of my Bar Mitzvah to come. So when my father announced that I could go with him to the Temple on the final day of the Feast of the Tabernacles, I was over the moon. What I couldn't understand was that my father seemed edgy, anxious even; when I spoke to him, he seemed distracted so in the end I asked him outright what was wrong.

He said it was all to do with Jesus.

'The man has this uncanny ability to draw crowds and hold their attention,' he said, 'way beyond anything I or my colleagues could match.'

Well, I didn't believe that for a minute. My father is about as high as you can get in the Sanhedrin and everyone respects him for his skill in teaching. Whereas this Jesus was a troublemaker; even I knew that. My father often had other members of the Sanhedrin to the house, and I was pretty good at eavesdropping on their conversations. I knew that they thought his teaching was outrageous and what's more, he performed miracles with absolutely no regard to the sanctity of the Sabbath. I knew that just the day before my father invited me to go with him, there had been uproar at the Temple and I asked my father to explain just what had happened.

I remember how he chewed his lip and frowned and then turned to me and began talking to me in a low voice.

'Jesus wanted to know why we were so angry that he healed someone on the Sabbath,' my father explained. 'And you know what he said? He said that we weren't making any sense, because we are very happy to circumcise a baby on the Sabbath, and that involves just one part of the body, but we don't like it if Jesus heals a man's whole body on the Sabbath.'

My father sighed deeply.

'Some of us tried to interrupt, but Jesus was in full flood, saying that it wasn't up to him to decide what he did or did not do, what he taught or said because everything was down to God who sent him. And then it happened.'

'What?' I asked.

'The crowd surged forward, pushing and shoving in an attempt to touch the hem of Jesus' robe and crying out that they believed.'

My father laid his hands on my shoulders.

'The vast majority of my friends want Jesus sorted once and for all,' he said. 'I think they even want him dead.'

Silence

Reflection of Nicodemus

On the last day of the Festival, I made a point of being in a prime position in the Temple as the priests processed waving palm branches. We had just reached the point in the worship where one of the priests carries a vessel of water from the Pool of Siloam up to the altar when Jesus began shouting.

'If anyone is thirsty, come to me! Anyone who believes in me and acknowledges who I am will have streams of life-giving water flowing through him, and spilling out of him – the Spirit of God . . .'

Well, at that the priests looked anything but holy and serene – they had faces like thunder, furious that the attention had moved from them to Jesus. They beckoned the Temple guards and my heart sank. They were going to seize him. I knew it.

But to my surprise, they didn't. You know what? I think they were frightened of the crowd. They hesitated for a while, then turned and marched straight out of the Temple. But I knew this wasn't the end of it.

And I was right. At the meeting of the Sanhedrin the following day, all the talk of was of arresting and sentencing Jesus to death.

Hymn

All you that pass by

Reading

John 7:50, 51

Nicodemus

I was shaking when I stood up to address the leader of the Sanhedrin, but I knew I could remain silent no longer. I demanded to know what part of our law condemns a man without first hearing him to find out what he is doing.

It was horrible. Even my closest friend turned on me, accusing me of losing my marbles, sneering and saying that maybe I was from Galilee too, since I was so smitten with this false prophet. I lost my cool; I reminded them of the blind man whom Jesus had healed just a few days earlier, a man whose parents admitted had never had one scrap of sight since birth but who could now see as clearly as I could. That man – uneducated and illiterate – said that Jesus had to have come from God to be able to do what he did and yet my colleagues – educated, well-read men of religion – couldn't take that on board.

I'll never forget the way they looked at me – some with pity, others with a downright sneer of contempt on their faces. I felt physically sick, knowing that some of them would shun me for evermore. And then suddenly, out of the blue, I remembered those words I had heard in the darkness three years before.

'For God so loved the world that he gave his one and only Son that whoever believes in him shall not perish but have eternal life.'

I took a deep breath, held up my hand, and to my surprise the room fell silent.

'Friends,' I said, 'our whole faith is founded on the belief that the Messiah will come. So why are we all finding it so hard to believe that he might just come in our own time?'

For one brief moment, I thought I had won them over. But I was wrong.

Choral anthem (where applicable)

For God so loved the world (Stainer)

or

Hymn

Love divine, all loves excelling *or* From heaven you came (*The Servant King*)

Reading

John 19:38-42

Nicodemus

My memory is not what it was. So much of those final weeks is now a blur, maybe because to remember every detail is too painful. But the end I will never forget.

They crucified him. I was there. I saw him die. I saw the soldier pierce his side and I saw the blood and water gush out. I saw the sun blotted out and darkness fall hours before it was time.

And it all came back to me.

Male voice (*from a different part of the church or worship space*)

He was despised and rejected of men, a man of sorrows and acquainted with grief . . . he was brought as a lamb to slaughter and as a sheep before its shearer is dumb. He was wounded for our transgressions, he was crushed for our iniquities; the punishment that brought us peace was on him and by his wounds we are healed. We all like sheep have gone astray, each of us has turned to his own way; and the Lord has laid on him the iniquity of us all.

Silence

Prayer

Lord Jesus Christ, you were despised, spat on, vilified – be with those today who face abuse and intolerance because of their beliefs, their race or their lifestyle. You were rejected – be with those today, we pray, who don't match up to society's expectations of what they should be, who don't fit the ideal of what it is to be successful or beautiful. Lord, you were acquainted with grief – be with all those today who mourn the loss of loved ones, of homeland, of employment and yes, of faith. Lord, you died that we might live: yet still we turn away. Turn away from those we find unattractive, from challenges that seem too hard to cope with, from a Lord who asks that day by day we should love as we all yearn to be loved. Forgive us, Lord, and as we come to you in repentance and faith, grant us through your grace, new vision, new determination and above all a fresh and unquenchable desire to do as you command in love, in faith and in hope. Amen.

Hymn

All I once held dear (*Knowing you*)

Nicodemus

My dear friend, Joseph of Arimathea, was the one who thought ahead and thought fast; he went to Pilate and somehow managed to get his permission for us to reclaim Jesus' body. I asked him what he planned to do with it and that's when he told me that he was giving his own new, unused tomb for Jesus. He said that he wanted to care for Jesus now in a way none of us did when he was alive – to bury him with dignity before the Sabbath.

He asked whether I would help. This time I didn't hesitate. I said yes at once and offered to provide the myrrh and aloes for the anointing of the body.

It seemed such a trivial thing. There was so much I should have said, so much I should have done – and now it was too late. Now it was all over. The man I now knew beyond a shadow of doubt was the Son of God was dead.

They say he came back to life. I never saw him, but hundreds of people did and they can't all be wrong. But why didn't I see him? I wish I had – for then I could be 100 per cent certain.

But maybe it's not about certainty. Maybe, after all, like he said, it's all about faith.

Prayers of intercession

Lord of life, forgive us when we refuse to acknowledge you openly for fear of what the world will think of us. Forgive us when we hesitate to testify to you because explaining seems too difficult. But Father, also forgive us when we do open our mouths – and only succeed in coming across as holier than thou or as having all the answers. Show us, we pray, how to speak your truth in words that people who do not yet know you can understand; never let us be ashamed to reveal our own faults and failings, or to share our own history of coming to faith, with all its doubts and pitfalls. And above all, gracious Lord, give us humility so that we realise we don't have all the answers, perseverance as we grapple with our understanding of Scripture, and joy in our hearts as we remember time and again that you never, ever give up on us. We pray it in Jesus' name. Amen.

(*Here follow intercessory prayers for the congregation, community and wider world.*)

Hymn

To God be the glory *or* We'll walk the land (*Let the flame burn brighter*)

Blessing and dismissal

5

All-age Advent service

This is suitable as a stand-alone short service or as the teaching slot in place of a sermon in a Eucharistic service. It also works well as a primary school assembly or for worship with children's groups.

Preparation

Before the service, hand out an envelope each to three children – a mixture of boys and girls. Tell them not to open them until they are requested. Each envelope will contain an invitation – The pink envelope will say 'Your best friend would like you to go to tea after school tomorrow'; the green envelope will have a message saying 'The Queen would like you to go to lunch next Saturday at Buckingham Palace'; the orange envelope will have a message saying 'You have been invited to play in goal for Manchester United next Saturday.' Three is the minimum number of envelopes, but if your congregation is large this can be increased to five with invitations such as 'you have been invited to present . . . (name a TV show)' or 'you have been invited to switch on the Christmas lights in your home town.'

It is suggested that a modern translation such as *The Message* or the Good News Bible is used for the readings appropriate to the Sunday on which the service is used.

Introduction

(Addressed to the children and young people.)

How many of you have a mobile phone? How many of you *would like to have* a mobile phone? Why? (*Hope for answers such as to keep in touch with friends, let people know where you are, etc.*)

How many of you are good at sending *text messages*? How many of the young people here think they are quicker at texting than their parents? What's so good about sending or receiving a text message? (*Listen to answers and encourage them to see that you don't have to reply to a text immediately; you can think about your options.*)

How many other ways can you think of that we get messages about important things? (*Emails, letters, Facebook, TV news bulletins, newspapers, school newsletter, etc., etc.,* ending with face-to-face *or, if that's been said earlier, reiterating it.*)

This morning, we are going to be thinking about messages – not just what they mean, but all the decisions and plans we have to make when we get them. But first we are going to sing our opening hymn.

Hymn

Long ago, prophets knew (*Ring bells, ring, ring, ring*)

Lighting of Advent candles

(*As the appropriate candle/candles are lit, the congregation will sing the appropriate verse of 'Christmas is coming, the Church is glad to sing'.*)

Depending on which Sunday in Advent, the following may be used:

First Sunday
Reading: Genesis 12:2-4; 26:4; 28:14
Explanation: Today we light a candle to remember the Patriarchs, faithful men who believed what God said, even when it sounded impossible. The lives of men like Abraham, Isaac and Jacob pointed to Jesus' life way in the future.

Second Sunday
Reading: Isaiah 60:1-3 and Matthew 24:44
Explanation: Today we remember the prophets of old, who delivered messages from God to the people and foretold the coming of the Christ child. Christ brought hope into a tired and troubled world and so this candle is often called the Hope candle. We light it now as a symbol of the prophets who remind us to be faithful and always keep hope alive for ourselves and others.

Third Sunday
Reading: Luke 3:1-6

Explanation: Today we remember John the Baptist, who came to prepare the way for Jesus, to be a messenger, to tell people to turn away from doing wrong and to live life in a new way.

Fourth Sunday

Reading: Luke 1:46-49

Explanation: Today we remember Mary, who was only a teenager when God chose her to bear his Son. Despite her fears and confusion, she knew that God's will was being fulfilled in her and that mattered far more than all the gossip, than all the uncertainty about the future and all the pain that saying 'Yes' to God would mean. We light this candle as a symbol of Mary and of her deep faith and commitment.

All these messages, down the centuries, pointed to one thing: the coming of Jesus as a baby who would grow up and become the Saviour of the world.

Hymn

Make way, make way

Second part of teaching

Sometimes we get messages that are very easy to believe. Sometimes we get messages that are not quite so easy to believe. When you arrived this morning, I gave three people an envelope. So would the person with the *pink* envelope stand up, open the envelope and tell us what it says?

('*Your best friend would like you to go to tea after school tomorrow.*')

Is that easy to believe? Yes. Is it easy to decide whether to say Yes or No?

Why is it easy? (*Listen to answers; hopefully because you like them, because you've been before and it was fun, etc.*) What would you have to do to get ready? (*Ask permission etc.*)

Now, would the person with the *green* envelope read what theirs says.

('*The Queen would like you to go to lunch next Saturday at Buckingham Palace.*')

Is that easy to believe? Not so easy. Why? (*Because the Queen doesn't know me, because I'm not important, because I'm just a kid, etc., etc.*)

So it's possible – perhaps the Queen has decided she wants to hear all about the latest chart toppers, or perhaps she just likes meeting children. It's possible – but not very likely. And if it was true, what would you have to do to get ready for *that* meeting? (*Take suggestions.*)

And now the person with the *orange* envelope.

(*'You have been asked to play in goal for Manchester United next Saturday.'*)

Is that one easy to believe? No. Why not? (*Because I'm not a member of the team, because I'm not good at football, etc.*)

So that is probably even less likely than getting an invitation to Buckingham Palace. But what if it was true? What would you have to do?

After our next song, we are going to hear about someone who got a very important message that was even harder to believe than playing for Man United, or going to Buckingham Palace. But first we will sing.

Hymn

Jesus bids us shine

Narrator	Once upon a time (all the best stories start that way), God needed to get a very important message to a girl called Mary. She lived in the village of Nazareth, and she was engaged to be married to a man called Joseph.
	Mary was busily sweeping, dusting and cleaning the house when suddenly she looked up and saw an angel standing in front of her.
Angel	Hello. You are a very special person, you know. A beautiful person. And God has a big surprise for you.
Narrator	Well, Mary was speechless. And actually she was just a little bit scared. After all, she hadn't seen an angel before and she didn't really know how you were supposed to talk to one. But the angel was very understanding.
Angel	There's nothing to be scared about. God's surprise is this: you are going to have a baby boy and you must call him Jesus.

Narrator	Well, at that point, Mary's mouth dropped open, she rubbed her eyes (just to make sure she wasn't seeing things) and she was just about to say something when she changed her mind. It would be rude to interrupt. So she didn't say 'Don't be so silly', or 'Get real.' She just went on listening.
Angel	This baby I'm talking about will be very special. He will be called Son of the Most High and he will rule forever and ever in his own special kingdom.
Narrator	Mary finally found her voice.
Mary	I don't get it. How can this possibly happen to someone like me? I'm not even married yet.
Angel	That doesn't matter because it's God who is going to make it happen. He's going to send his Holy Spirit down to you and that's how you will get pregnant.
Narrator	Now the angel could see that Mary was having just a little bit of trouble getting her head round this, so he gave her another rather amazing piece of news.
Angel	Your cousin Elizabeth is also going to have a child.
Narrator	Now you may think that was no big deal, but Elizabeth was very old, far too old to have a baby. But you see, with God, nothing is impossible.
	That's when it all clicked in Mary's head.
Mary	I see. Now I understand. This is *God's* plan. OK. I'm ready to do what he wants.
Narrator	No sooner had she agreed than the angel disappeared and Mary was left alone. And she was never quite the same again. We are now going to sing a song that is all about the message that the angel gave to Mary. (*If appropriate, have one side of the church/hall singing the question, and the other the answer.*)

Hymn

Now tell us, gentle Mary

Prayers

(The response is: *Help us to listen, trust and obey.*)

Thank you, God, for choosing Mary to be the mother of Jesus. We know that sometimes you have important things for us to do. When they seem too difficult or scary, remind us that you are right beside us and will always give us the strength we need.

Help us to listen, trust and obey.

We are sorry, Lord, for the times when we say spiteful things, or behave in ways that are unkind or thoughtless. Thank you so much for forgiving us and please, Lord, when you ask us to forgive others:

Help us to listen, trust and obey.

As we prepare for Christmas, there are so many exciting things going on. We pray for all those children and families who have very little to look forward to, all who are hungry, homeless or suffering pain or sickness. Thank you for doctors, nurses, carers and aid agencies who help to bring light and hope into dark places. Show us, Father, ways in which we too can be of help.

Help us to listen, trust and obey. Amen.

The Lord's Prayer

Hymn

How lovely on the mountain (*Our God reigns*)

Blessing and dismissal

6

The crowd

A service for Advent

Introduction

There are many people in the Gospels whose stories are very familiar to us: John the Baptist, Mary and Joseph, Zechariah, the disciples, Lazarus, Mary and Martha . . . but what of the others? What of those people referred to time and again simply as 'the crowd'? Today, we are able to read about the whole of Jesus' ministry – many of the Galileans of his time may only have spoken to him once or merely heard him teach on one occasion. Some would have been in the crowd for just a day or so, when Jesus visited their home village; others might have decided to stick with him for a month, a year or even longer.

Some we know about even though we don't know their names: the healed lepers, the woman with the haemorrhage, the boy with the loaves and fishes. Others are just bystanders in the story, nameless members of the crowd who followed him, listened to him, waved palm branches for him and finally watched him die.

How were their lives changed by their encounter with Christ? We can only imagine; maybe some felt compelled to live in a different way, while others were too hidebound by convention to see beyond the fact that Jesus was turning all the rules and regulations upside down and challenging their whole world. Maybe some left the crowd because they couldn't meet Jesus' penetrating gaze and perhaps, almost certainly, yet more left only because they wanted to run at full speed and tell others what they had seen and heard.

And what of us? Has our encounter with the living Christ changed us so much that we have to get out there and share the good news with others? Or does the culture we live in make us wary of speaking out; do we feel more comfortable keeping our faith to ourselves rather than risk being challenged or ridiculed? Do we want to cherry pick the bits of Christ's teaching that fit comfortably with our plans for our life and our future, or are we willing to go wherever the voice of God calls us to go?

What of us this Advent season? Are we waiting passively for Christmas and the familiarity of the Nativity story, or are we actively expecting God to work in our lives in new and challenging ways?

What of us indeed?

Hymn

Jesus calls us o'er the tumult *or* It's rising up *or* O God of burning, cleansing flame (*Send the fire*)

Reading

John 2:1-11

Reflection of an unknown follower

Am I a follower of Jesus? Yes I am. But I am not proud of what got me started on this extraordinary journey. Certainly the emotions that motivated me were not feelings to be proud of: greed, envy, a desire for wealth – all the things that were the exact opposite of what Jesus looked for in believers. But back then, the day it started – well I was just a kid on the make.

I ran away straight after the wedding. Running away is what I did in those days – away from my father, away from our rat-infested shack, away from the terrible thing I had done. I guess back then I hadn't discovered that the one thing you can't run away from is yourself.

Anyway, there was no way I was going to stay in that dead-end job, waiting on other people after what I saw the man Jesus do. It was mind-blowing. What happened was this: right in the middle of the wedding feast, just when the guests were getting into the swing of things, the wine ran out. To be honest, the steward had been grumbling all week, saying that the bridegroom was more interested in inviting huge numbers of guests than he was in providing enough for them to eat and drink, but I took no notice. He's the kind of guy who isn't happy unless he can find something to moan about. Trouble was, he was also the type of man who blames everyone but himself for any mishap. So when I went to refill some pitchers and realised that the very last drop of wine had gone, I was at my wits' end.

The other servants kept coming up for refills and the guests were beginning to tap their fingers impatiently on the tables. That's when this elderly lady beckoned me over. At first I pretended not to notice, assuming that she wanted more of what we no longer had; but she was persistent, and she was smiling and after all, I was just the paid servant – so I went.

'Is there a problem?' she asked gently. 'You all seem a bit agitated.'

Well, that was a turn up – to the majority of the guests, we servants were just there to serve; our feelings weren't their problem. I was so taken aback that I answered her almost without thinking of the consequences.

'The wine has run out, Madam.'

'I see,' she said and with that, she got up. For one awful moment, I thought she was going to go straight to the master, so I scuttled back into the kitchen to keep a safe distance from the eruption I was sure was coming. But as I watched, I saw that it wasn't the master she was heading for but the far corner of the courtyard where a group of young guys were laughing and joking, making more noise than the rest of the gathering put together. She began talking earnestly to one particular man who shook his head several times, and then threw his arms in the air in defeat, stood up and followed her straight to the kitchen.

'Do what my son Jesus says,' the woman said softly. Then she walked back to her seat and began chatting to her neighbour.

This Jesus turned to me and a couple of the other servants.

'Fill those jars with water,' he told us, pointing to the six stone water jars lined up by the wall.

He's crazy, I thought to myself. Rowdy guests were hardly going to take that lying down.

'And now,' he said to me when the jars were brimming, 'draw some out and take it to the steward.'

It was all I could do to hold my tongue. Taking a jug of water to the steward at this stage in the feast and announcing that that was all there was to drink – he'd hit the roof and blame anyone but himself for the miscalculation. But he was a guest and we had to do as we were told.

I stepped forward, began pouring some of the water into a pitcher – and promptly dropped it on the floor.

The jar was full of wine.

I assume I took the wine to the steward. I imagine I refilled goblets and took fresh orders. All I recall looking back is that my mind began racing. Here was a man who could magically turn water into wine. I didn't know how he did it, but I knew I wanted to learn the trick.

When I heard Jesus say he was leaving for Capernaum, I knew what I had to do. In the dead of night I left that house and set out, determined to catch up with him and get him to teach me the tricks of his trade. And before I went I pocketed the few things I had managed to pinch during the wedding. People are so careless with their possessions when the wine is flowing freely.

Hymn

Songs of thankfulness and praise

Reading

Mark 1:30-34

Unknown follower

It wasn't the way I thought it would be. I thought I'd catch up with Jesus, talk to him and persuade him to teach me his magic. I hadn't bargained for the size of the crowd that followed him – not just poor people like me but wealthy types, all desperate to hear him speak about some kingdom he was going to set up. Apparently it was going to be a new kingdom, where the Romans would be overthrown and everyone would be free. It sounded pretty good to me.

And I hadn't realised that Jesus didn't just turn water into wine – he cured diseases. There was this woman – the mother-in-law of one of his best mates – who was burning up with fever, and he just took hold of her hand and hey presto! She was leaping about doing the cooking. You think I'm kidding? I was only half a furlong away – I saw it happen.

Well, of course, more and more people came to find him. There were folk being carried on stretchers, blind people being led by the hand, kids fitting and frothing at the mouth – and he cured them. Just like that.

This was one amazing man.

But try as hard as I did, I couldn't get anywhere near to Jesus; everywhere he went his cronies went with him, and even when I got close, they would take one look at me, see that there was nothing wrong with me and shoo me away.

Then things really hotted up. I had got closer to Jesus than ever before when suddenly there was the sound of a bell. A cry went through the crowd, and people scattered, shouting and swearing. Some of them turned tail and ran away, others brandished their staffs and shouted 'Go away!' at the tops of their voices.

It didn't take long to see why. A leper was shuffling through the crowd, his hand bandaged in filthy rags, his nose eaten away, his face distorted with huge pustules. His feet were deformed by the disease; one eye was closed tight. And let me tell you, he didn't smell so good either.

And he was heading straight for Jesus.

Silence

Hymn

Heaven shall not wait

or

Taizé chant

O Lord, hear my prayer

Reading

Mark 1:40-45

Reflection of the leper

It was a long shot, I knew that. I don't mean that I didn't believe Jesus could cure me; I was pretty sure that he could. But I didn't think they would let me come within a mile of the man, unclean as I was.

Everywhere I go, people flee; I live, with all the others like me, by the town dump outside the walls and when I do get near anyone, the only expression I see on their faces is one of utter revulsion. So, no, I didn't think I had a hope in hell of getting close to Jesus.

But I had to try.

His disciples tried to drive me away – but Jesus held up his hand, glared at them and beckoned me closer. My heart was thudding in my chest, my mouth was as dry as a bone but I made myself look him in the eye.

The gaze of tenderness that I saw there made me want to weep. I fell to my knees and forced the words from my twisted and sore-encrusted mouth.

'Lord, if you want to, I know you can make me clean.'

Jesus smiled at me.

'Of course I want to,' he said. And then – and you won't believe this, but I swear it is true. He touched me. Jesus touched *me* – a leper. That's against the law – and it meant that in the eyes of everyone else, Jesus himself was now unclean.

The whole crowd gasped, and his disciples looked at him as if he had taken leave of his senses. Jesus ignored them and gestured to me to get to my feet. As I stood up the gasps were even louder.

I hardly dared believe it. I ran my fingers over my face – the pustules had gone. The skin was smooth. Suddenly the world seemed twice as bright and I realised that my left eye was now wide open. I pulled off my bandages and my hands were without blemish, the twisted fingers straight and strong.

'Master!' That was the only word I could manage as the sobs constricted my throat.

Jesus smiled at me and rested a hand on my shoulder.

'Now listen to me,' he said. 'You are not to tell anyone about this – no one at all. Your first job is to go straight to the priest and make the sacrifice demanded by the law.'

I nodded but, to be honest, I hardly took it in. I kept twirling round, gazing at my hands, putting my full weight on feet that until a moment ago had been twisted and gnarled.

'Go now,' Jesus said. 'And remember, not a word to anyone.'

I didn't get that – and even now, years on, I don't. I mean, surely Jesus would want the whole world to know what he had done? Why keep it a secret? I did go to the priest – and I did tell anyone who would listen.

And the oddest thing of all was that, months later, when I had got a job of sorts and was earning my keep and not being shunned in the street, it wasn't enough. Oh, I don't mean I wasn't grateful and happy – but I yearned to know more, to feel again that – well, yes, I'll say it – that love that emanated from Jesus when he looked at me.

That's why I found out where he was and that's why I followed him. Oh, I had lapses, times when I needed to earn some money and had to linger in a village until I could get some piecework, but I always caught up with him. I listened to his stories, to his teaching. And I'm here now. Outside Pilate's palace. Waiting for them to release him.

Because they'll have to, won't they? Who could have anything against a man like that?

Silence

Prayer

Lord Jesus Christ, so often we pray that you would help us to reach out to the dispossessed, to those whose lifestyles and values seem contrary to everything the world values. Whether through inbuilt fears of contagion, or our own preconceived prejudices, we find excuses not to engage. We ask you to help us to see the world through your eyes and yet when we are confronted with people whose lives have brought them to the lowest places, we want to turn away because we do not know what to do. Open our hearts, fill us with courage when we meet the homeless, the diseased, the desperate and the mentally ill, and remind us that when we turn away from them, we turn away from you. We pray this in your name and trusting in your strength. Amen.

Hymn

Jesus Christ is waiting *or* Jesus, you are changing me

Reading

Mark 5:25-34

Reflection of the woman with the haemorrhage

Twelve years I had been ill. Twelve long years – and it wasn't the type of illness that one talked about. I bled three weeks out of every four, I had no energy and the pain was dreadful. I just wanted to die. There was no money left for doctors – all that went years ago. And for what? No improvement and no chance of a social life – I couldn't go near a man, I couldn't go into a public place. I was an outcast.

There seemed to be no reason to live.

Of course, I'd heard about Jesus; who hadn't? I thought that if anyone could help me, it would be him. But how could I go and find him? I was bleeding even more heavily with every passing week. I could have wept – there he was, only a few miles away, this healer, this curer of all ills, and I couldn't go near him because he was a man and I was unclean.

That's when the anger took over. It wasn't fair: I'd heard he touched a leper, so clearly he wasn't bothered about the rules and regulations. Of course, the leper had been a man but still . . .

Then one day I was staggering back from the well (there's only so long you can go without water, ill or not) and I overheard two men talking. Of course, I dodged behind a wall because I didn't want to be seen but I could hear what they said quite clearly. They were saying that Jesus turned all the rules upside down – turned on its head everything that society said was right. And one of them said he was taking a terrible risk.

And you know what? Something in my head said 'Why don't you take a risk too?'

And the following day, he came to our village. I saw the crowd and I went out and there he was. I knew I couldn't speak to him – I wasn't that brave – but as he walked by I felt this huge tug in my heart, the urge to be close to him. I don't know what took hold of me but I went forward and I touched his robe.

It stopped. No really, it did. Just like that. That dreadful ache in my loins, the gushing from my body, all stopped in an instant.

And so did Jesus. Stopped dead in his tracks and looked into the crowd.

'Who touched me?' he asked. Well, you can imagine, I was terrified. One of his disciples laughed and pointed out that with the crowd the way it was a dozen elbows could have been nudging him. But Jesus just shook his head and said that he knew for sure someone had touched him and that power had gone out of him.

And all of a sudden it seemed as if the people around him had melted away and there he was in front of me and I had no escape. So I knelt down and admitted it was me – and said that I knew I was cured.

The words he spoke to me still make me cry. He said 'daughter' – yes, he called me, Hannah, the unclean woman, daughter! 'Daughter,' he said, 'the faith and the courage that brought you to me have given you healing and health. Go now and live in peace.'

Jesus treated me as though I was worth something – he never once said I shouldn't have touched him. It was as if I was more important than the rules.

I didn't know how to thank him, but recently I've found a way. I'm poor when it comes to money or property, but there is one thing I can do. Tell people what happened to me; tell them that Jesus' rules are not like the ones our leaders make; tell them that everyone, rich or poor, sick or well, clever or ignorant matter to him. I discovered that in the space of five minutes and I will spend the rest of my days on earth helping others to discover it too.

Silence

Prayer

Lord, let us never be too fearful to reach out to you. When we have no words to pray, may we hold you in our hearts; when we have too much pain to express, may we lay it at your feet. And may we know, deep in our hearts, that each one of us, flawed and fearful as we are, is your child, loved, understood and welcomed into your loving arms. Amen.

Hymn

I want to walk with Jesus Christ (*Follow him, follow him*)

Reflection of the unknown follower

'Jesus I need to talk to you.'

Nearly three years I'd been dipping in and out of the crowd that followed him and it had taken me all that time to pluck up the courage. I'd seen him restore sight to the blind, make cripples walk and the possessed regain their senses. He'd fed a vast crowd with a few measly loaves and a couple of fish and, if the rumours were to be believed, he'd even calmed a violent storm just by telling the wind to calm down.

I had long since stopped thinking of him as a magician; he was a man of God – some said he was God's own Son. All I know is that the longer I followed him, the more the shame and the guilt about my past ate away at me. He talked about repenting of our sins and frankly, I didn't know how. What did that mean? I couldn't undo all the stealing and the cheating and the other bad things too horrible to mention; so was I a write-off in his eyes? I had to know.

'Jesus I need to talk to you.'

I trembled as I said the words to him and he just smiled.

'I know you do,' he said. 'But first, come with me. I have a story I want to tell you all.'

Frankly, I was a bit miffed. I didn't want yet another story – I wanted him to listen to me. But I did what he said. And I listened to the story.

Reading

Luke 15:11-32 (*This can be read or enacted as the situation demands.*)

Unknown follower

Afterwards, he turned to me.

'Now do you understand?' he said. 'Nothing you have done can ever make your Father in heaven love you less. He never gives up yearning and waiting and longing for those people who are lost to come back to him. And when they do – well, his joy is beyond words and his forgiveness is total and absolute.'

I said nothing. I was struggling not to cry.

He looked at me.

'Do you have a good memory?' he asked.

I nodded. 'I guess so,' I said.

'Then remember the stories I have told you and all the ones I will continue to tell until the day when I have to leave you – remember them and tell them to others. Tell them to people your age and younger; tell them to those who believe they are beyond love and beyond help.'

'Me? Tell your stories?' I asked.

He nodded.

'Take who you are, and what you've been through, and what you've learned from me and use it all in the service of the Father who created you and loves you.'

So that's what I'm doing. Some people listen, many don't. But I won't shut up because for the first time in my life, I'm doing what I know is right. And it's a good feeling.

Prayers of intercession for the congregation, community and wider world

Hymn

Lord, for the years *or* Jesus, take me as I am

Blessing and dismissal

7

I so don't get it

Reflection of an unchurched teenager

This reflection is designed to be used as a teaching/meditation tool for youth groups, confirmation candidates, explorers and enquirers. However, it would work well within the framework of a Eucharistic service for youth that thinks out of the box. I have made suggestions for hymns and worship songs and the response of the narrator will indicate the type of hymn that would fit the slot should those using it wish to make changes. And lastly, this is not a reflection to be taken at high speed!

Teen   I haven't been in one of these places for years. Not since my nan's funeral when I was just a kid. I don't know why I'm here really. Well, yes, I do – I'm here because a church is the one place where he wouldn't even think of looking for me. Especially when to get here he'd have to pass the pub and he's never walked by one of those in years. I'm sitting in a corner as far away from the door as I possibly can just in case he does come. Which he won't. Please God, he won't.

That woman over there is giving me funny looks. She's whispering to her friend – now they're both staring. Maybe this wasn't such a clever idea – maybe I should just go and take my chances . . .

Oh no, it's starting. I'll just keep my head down and look like I do this kind of thing every week.

Leader   The Lord be with you.

Congregation   *And also with you.*

Hymn

Joy to the world *or* I come with joy, a child of God

Teen   They don't *look* very joyful. In fact half of them look as miserable as I feel. Perhaps they're all hiding from stuff as well. I wonder.

Prayer of preparation

Congregation   *Almighty God, to whom all hearts are open, all desires known and from whom no secrets are hidden . . .*

Teen   That's scary. Like – God knows all of it? He knows how I hate my dad, how I pinch stuff from shops because my mum's sick and my little sister still believes in Santa Claus? How I lie awake at nights dreading the sound of his footsteps on the stairs? Like I plan ways that I could kill him without ever getting found out?

Congregation   *Cleanse the thoughts of our hearts . . .*

Teen   Now hang on. I get it – I'm supposed to forgive my dad for beating my mum and for – well, for all the stuff he does to me? I'm supposed to 'think beautiful thoughts', right? Well, I can't. I knew I shouldn't have come. These places are unreal.

Congregation   *By the inspiration of your Holy Spirit . . .*

Teen   I never did get the Holy Spirit. We did him at school but like – he – it – is invisible. Just like God and Jesus really – talked about a lot but you never get to see them face-to-face, you never get to have them explain stuff. Just RE teachers and vicars and people like that who talk in posh voices and peer at you and never answer the difficult questions.

Congregation   *That we may perfectly love you . . .*

Teen   I haven't done anything perfectly ever. My dad says I'm a total waste of space, my school tutor says I'm wasting my God-given potential . . . actually, that's a laugh because if God gave me potential why did he go and muck up my life so that I couldn't study even if I wanted to? Why did he make Dad a bully and give Mum all those illnesses and the mental stuff and make my little sister so scared that she wets the bed and hides in cupboards? Know what? I find it pretty hard to love someone who can call himself God and then let all that stuff happen.

Congregation *And worthily magnify your holy name . . .*

Teen Which I guess means go around saying how great God is and never swearing. Well, that's me done then. Great. One prayer and they've made it quite clear that this is no place for someone like me. I am so out of here. I mean it. I'm not stopping.

Congregation *Through Christ our Lord. Amen.*

Teen That vicar guy smiled at me. Why did he smile at me? Oh God, he's looking straight at me. And he's still smiling. This is freaking me out.

Leader When the Lord comes, he will bring to light the things now hidden in darkness, and will disclose the purposes of the heart. Therefore in the light of Christ let us confess our sins.

Teen You so have to be joking! Out loud – tell this lot what I've done and said and thought? Like that's ever going to happen. Still, I can't leave yet because it's all gone quiet and the church door is like hundreds of years old and creaks. So I'd better just kneel here and pretend I care.

Leader Most merciful God, Father of our Lord Jesus Christ . . .

Teen You know, I never got that. For ages I thought Joseph was the dad. We did Nativity plays at school – not that I ever got any of the good parts. I've been a sheep, a camel and a star – all the rubbishy parts for kids whose mums couldn't or wouldn't make wings out of coat hangers or sew robes with beads stuck on them. The Angel Gabriel was always someone with long blond hair and a posh voice who had to say that Mary would have a baby and she had to call him Jesus. Which seemed like a bit of a cheek to me because what if Mary didn't like that name? Anyway, later on in RE we got told that actually Joseph wasn't the father – it was God. How that happened I haven't a clue. I know the facts of life. Our teacher said it was a miracle; but actually, I think it's a bit scary – I mean, what if Mary hadn't wanted to be Jesus' mum? Could she have said no? Or was she brainwashed into a kind of zombie-like 'OK, then'? They never tell you that stuff in RE.

Leader   We confess that we have sinned in thought . . .

Teen   Hang on a minute – surely it doesn't count as a sin if you just think it? Does it? So when I think about how great it would be if my dad dropped dead so he wouldn't be around to beat my mum and come to my room at night and . . . you mean, God thinks that's a sin?

Leader   word . . .

Teen   Yeah, well OK, that makes more sense. Like when I told that lie about my best mate and the guy at the corner shop, or called Amanda a slag because she took Justin off me (well, he dumped me actually but it was easier to blame her). Yes, I get the bit about confessing spoken sins.

Leader   and deed . . .

Teen   Like the shoplifting and the booze and the skiving off school. Only the thing is, which is worse? Sinning by stealing a present for my little sister – or letting her be the only kid at nursery who didn't get anything? Having a drink or two to make the pain go away or hurting so much that I lash out at the first person who says hi to me? Missing school to stay home with my sister and make sure she's safe when Mum's having one of her bad days – or leaving a 4-year-old to cope alone?

Leader   We have not loved you with our whole heart . . .

Teen	How can I love someone who doesn't do anything to help?
Leader	We have not loved our neighbours as ourselves . . .
Teen	You haven't met our neighbours. They're not easy to love. And anyway I don't love myself; I hate me, so that doesn't work.
Leader	In your mercy forgive what we have been . . .
Teen	Like the bits I don't dare think about – like the money I took from that guy asleep on the bus and the time I threw a brick through Mr Conway's window because he'd called the police about my dad and my dad thought it was me and hurt me worse than ever before.
Leader	help us to amend what we are . . .
Teen	What am I? A no good waste of space according to my dad. But I'd like to be good and laid back and not scared all the time, and if you, God, could do that it would be cool. Hey what am I on? I'm talking to God like he's really there and listening.
Leader	and direct what we shall be . . .
Teen	If I don't get my act together, I'll be stuck in a dead-end job. That's what my form tutor says. But if you can make things happen, God, I'd really like to be a nursery nurse. Make life better for little kids like my sister.
Leader	That we may do justly, love mercy and walk humbly with you, our God.
Teen	Ah. That's the catch then – 'our' God. The God of people like this lot – not that I'd call all of them humble. Some of them seem totally up themselves, looking sideways at me with my piercings and my tattoos. Now what? The vicar's standing up and looking right at me again. He's smiling – what's so funny? I bet he thinks it's a right laugh that someone like me is here. I'm going . . .

Leader	Almighty God, who forgives all who truly repent . . .
Teen	Repent? Does that mean being sorry for being like you are? And if it does, why don't they say so?
Leader	have mercy upon you, pardon and deliver you from all your sins . . .
Teen	Can he do that? Not just forgive but actually take away all the anger and the pain that makes me lash out and do bad things?
Leader	confirm and strengthen you in all goodness . . .
Teen	I'd like to be good. I've tried. It doesn't work. The badness always comes back. Even a little bit of goodness would be nice, then people might like me more and I'd really like to be liked.
Leader	and keep you in life eternal . . .
Teen	I don't want eternal life. Well, not like the one I've got right now. What is eternal life anyway? If everyone lives forever, heaven must be a pretty crowded place and it's not up in the sky like my gran used to say because satellites and rockets and things have never found it, have they? I wonder where it is and what people do there for eternity? I'd like to ask the vicar that – I wonder if I dare?
Leader	through Jesus Christ our Lord.
Congregation	*Amen.*
Teen	Amen – that means 'so be it'. I know that from school. Well, OK, God: *so be it*. Make me nice, make my dad go away and never come back, make Mum better, look after Mandy . . . *Amen. Amen. Amen*. So like – do it, OK?

The Kyries

Leader	Lord Jesus, you came to gather the nations into the peace of your kingdom.

Teen	Well, that's not happening, is it?
Congregation	*Kyrie eleison, Christe eleison, Kyrie eleison.*
Teen	Now what? They're singing in some foreign language. Why can't they do it in English?
Leader	You come in word and sacrament to strengthen us in holiness.
Teen	You need a flippin' dictionary to understand this lot.
Congregation	*Lord have mercy, Christ have mercy, Lord have mercy.*
Teen	Oh God, now I'm going to cry! Why am I going to cry? It's that word – mercy. It makes me think of someone wrapping their arms round me and rocking me, and telling me it's all going to be all right. Not that anyone's done that for a long time, not since my nan died. She used to say 'Mercy me, my little precious lambkin, now what's wrong?' and cuddle me and say she loved me and . . . I miss her so much.
Leader	You will come in glory with salvation for your people.
Teen	The woman across the aisle has just passed me a tissue. Now I feel like a right idiot – I'll sneeze a bit and pretend I've got a cold. Oh good, they're all sitting down and someone's going up to read. I can wait till that's over and then slip away.

First reading

Isaiah 40:1-11

Teen	That was like poetry. I didn't know the Bible could sound like that. I didn't get it all, but I liked the bit about comfort, and speaking tenderly and penalties being paid. I kind of switched off after that because it made my chest go all tight and I wanted to cry again. Wouldn't it be so so cool if life could really be like that? The only other bit I heard properly was about

71

lambs being gathered into his arms – I did that once at primary school when we went on a farm trip, and it was lovely. I buried my nose in the lamb's fleece and it was all warm and wriggly. So are they saying God wants to do that with us?

Gospel reading

Teen   Hey, now what? The vicar's walking down the aisle – is it over? Can we go now? I guess we can because everyone's turned round to see him go and . . . no. He's stopping. He's going to read again.

Leader   Hear the Gospel of our Lord Jesus Christ according to N.

Congregation *Glory to you, O Lord.*

Teen   It's the story about the angel coming to tell Mary she's going to have a baby. And what's more he's reading it in proper English, without all the Thee and Thou bits. Neat. I bet Mary was terrified. I know the Bible doesn't say she was, but I guess the people that wrote it thought that she was meant to be holy and holy people don't get frightened by angels. I wish angels were real: I mean, nowadays – obviously they were then because she saw one.

   Now the vicar's going up into the pulpit and I can't leave because everyone's sitting down and they'll stare if I go.

Sermon

Teen   Wow. I got that. And it was dead short which was good. When he said, 'Welcome to all our visitors,' he looked right at me and grinned. Not an up-himself grin, a really friendly one. Then he talked about how Christmas is a confusing time because everyone is meant to be really happy, and yet sometimes it's the

72

saddest time of the whole year for people who feel lonely or different or unloved.

He said that it didn't matter if you lived in a house that was always a mess because the stable was pretty grotty too; and it didn't matter if you couldn't afford big presents for people because the shepherds didn't take anything to the stable, only the Three Kings and they were rich so probably it wouldn't have been an effort for them. He said caring and loving were the important things and looking out for people who couldn't look out for themselves. That made me think of Mandy – my little sister – and I nearly blubbed all over again.

Affirmation of faith

Leader   Let us declare our faith in God.

Congregation   *We believe in God the Father, from whom every family in heaven and on earth is named . . .*

Teen   I don't know if I do believe in him, but I guess I must a bit because I talked to him.

Congregation   *We believe in God the Son, who lives in our hearts through faith, and fills us with his love . . .*

Teen   I don't know if I do believe in him, but I guess I must a bit because I'm here, aren't I? And I could have left, I guess.

Congregation   *We believe in God the Holy Spirit, who strengthens us with power from on high . . .*

Teen   I definitely don't know if I believe in him . . . except that I feel better than I did when I got here, kind of stronger and safer. Only a bit but . . .

Congregation   *We believe in one God; Father, Son and Holy Spirit. Amen.*

Intercessions

Teen   Let them pray for the Queen and the government and the United Nations and all that – I just want . . . well, if you're there, God, and if you can hear me, can you sort out the mess of my life? Turn my dad away from the booze and make Mum well again in her head. Can you sort out the muddle with the benefits and make the council do something about the damp on the bedroom wall? Can you make sure Mandy is OK? Can you make people listen when I tell them that time's running out for Mandy – he'll start on her if someone doesn't do something soon. Please God. Make someone come and care. And make it soon. Amen.

The Peace

Teen   I so don't want to do this. Everyone's shaking hands and hugging and that is so not me. Oh God. *Hi. What? Oh. Yeah, like hello. Peace?* I wish. Go away – oh no, there's another one. *Me? Lisa. Yeah, it's my first time for ages. Peace. Coffee? After? Well, no . . . I . . . peace. Peace be with you.* That was weird – two people shook my hand and didn't stare at the skull tattoo on my wrist or my eyebrow piercings. That's weird – I thought they'd freak out.

Leader   And now we will sing our offertory hymn . . .

Offertory hymn

Teen   I haven't got much cash and what I have got I need. I want to get Mandy a stocking because she still believes in Santa Claus . . . I'll put 5p in. I hope they don't notice how little it is.

Hymn

Do not offer me your money *or* Christ's is the world (*A touching place*)

At the preparation of the table

Leader   Blessed are you, Lord, God of all creation; through your goodness we have these and all our gifts to offer, the fruit of our labour and of the skills you have given us. Take us and our possessions to do your work in the world. Blessed be God for ever.

Teen   I guess God has given this lot loads of stuff, so they can chuck five-pound notes in the collection bag. And I bet they've all got loads of skills, and high-powered jobs, and houses of their own with posh furniture like you see in the DFS adverts. But I haven't, God, and, what's more, it's your fault. If you're the one handing out cleverness and dosh, how come I didn't get any? How do you choose who to give stuff to and who to turn your back on? This is winding me up. I'm getting angry now.

Leader   The Lord is here.

Congregation   *His Spirit is with us.*

Teen   It must be nice to be like these people, and be so sure that God's with you because you've got life sussed and know how to fit in.

Leader   Lift up your hearts.

Congregation   *We lift them to the Lord.*

Teen   OK, God, I'm going to give you one last chance, OK? I've told you stuff that I don't tell anyone, if that's what lifting up your heart means. So what are you going to do about it?

Leader   Let us give thanks to the Lord our God.

Congregation   *It is right to give thanks and praise.*

Teen   I don't know what I'm supposed to give thanks for. Except, I guess, Mandy getting to go to that sleepover with Annie – that's a big thank you, because Annie's mum is dead nice and their house is always warm and they have a hot meal every day. So yeah, thanks for that. And for my paper round – I like walking in the streets and just thinking. Thanks for that.

Leader   It is indeed right and good to give you thanks and praise, almighty God and everlasting Father, through Jesus Christ your Son. For when he humbled himself to come among us in human flesh, he fulfilled the plan you formed before the foundation of the world . . .

Teen   Do you have plans for everyone, God, or just the important people? If it's everyone, could you plan something that gets me away from home? Please. Except then Mandy would be on her own and he . . . no, that wouldn't work. Could you plan something that makes home a better place to be?

Leader   . . . to open for us the way of salvation. Confident that your promise will be fulfilled, we now watch for the day when Christ our Lord will come again in glory.

Teen   That's scary. I don't want to think about that. I mean, if he did come back he would so not want to know me. Anyway, they've been saying he'll come back for 2000 years and he hasn't done it, so I guess he's hardly going to pop up next Friday, is he? Is he? But if he did . . . well, if he did he'd go and hang out with the posh people. Only he didn't first time round, did he? He ended up in a smelly, dirty stable. I guess if he wanted smelly and grubby, he might just pick a house like mine. Now that is one freaky thought.

Leader   And so we join our voices with angels and archangels and with all the company of heaven to proclaim your glory, for ever praising you and singing:
Father, we worship you, everlasting and almighty:

Congregation   *Father, we worship you, everlasting and almighty.*

Teen   I like singing. I'm good at it too – I know I am. When I sing, I feel different inside. It must be lovely to be in the choir here and get to sing every week. Not that they'd have someone like me – I've seen a couple of those old ones staring at my nose ring. If they saw the stud in my tongue, they'd probably pass out!

Leader We praise and bless you, loving Father, through Jesus Christ our Lord: and as we obey his command, send your Holy Spirit, that broken bread and wine out-poured may be for us the body and blood of your dear Son.

Teen That is seriously weird. Like, it's a piece of bread and a mug of wine – how can they expect me to believe it's flesh and blood and even if I did, that would be horrendously gut-wrenchingly awful. That cross with Jesus hanging on it – I mean, how can they bear to look at that every Sunday? Although perhaps they're so used to it being there that they don't notice it any more. It shouldn't be gold, though. It should be wooden, like the one in that film about Jesus that was on TV.

Leader On the night before he died he had supper with his friends . . .

Teen That makes him sound normal, like a regular guy. Supper with his friends. I wonder what they had to eat.

Leader . . . and taking bread, he praised you. He broke the bread, gave it to them and said: Take, eat; this is my body which is given for you; do this in remembrance of me.

Teen That makes more sense. That reminds me of my nan. Every 25 March, on my grandad's birthday, she baked apple cake because it was his favourite. Never mind that he was dead – she carried on doing it and she always iced it and wrote 'For Fred' in wonky letters. In remembrance of him. So I guess that Jesus wanted his mates to have a meal together to remind them of the times they shared. I like that. That's the kind of thing I can get my head around.

Leader   When supper was ended he took the cup of wine. Again he praised you, gave it to them and said: Drink this, all of you; this is my blood of the new covenant, which is shed for you and for many for the forgiveness of sins. Do this, as often as you drink it, in remembrance of me.

Teen   What's a covenant? And how come drinking wine gets us forgiven? Not that I can drink it anyway because I'm not a church person.

Leader   Jesus, we worship you, everlasting and almighty:

Congregation *Jesus, we worship you, everlasting and almighty.*

Leader   So Father, we remember all that Jesus did . . .

Teen   I do remember bits – things we learned at primary school, like when he fed 5000 people with a couple of fish and a few loaves of bread, and the time when he brought that little girl back from the dead. Trouble is, stuff like that doesn't happen any more does it? It's just a nice story, a bit like Cinderella and Sleeping Beauty.

Leader   in him we plead with confidence . . .

Teen   Confidence? Does that mean we can beg him for things and know for absolute certain we'll get them? I doubt it – it's never worked for me before. I suppose you have to join their church club before you can get in line for the handouts.

Leader   . . . his sacrifice made once for all upon the cross.

Teen   I had an argument with my RE teacher about that. I said how could one man getting crucified 2000 years ago mean that every bad person in the world got forgiven, even if they weren't born at the time, and even if they didn't like Jesus. She told me to be quiet and get on with my work. Which meant she didn't have an answer. I wonder if this vicar guy can do any better? If I dared ask, which I don't.

Leader	Bringing before you the bread of life and the cup of salvation, we proclaim his death and resurrection until he comes in glory . . .
Teen	What exactly does resurrection mean? I told my RE teacher I wanted to come back as a rich kid and she went ballistic; how was I supposed to know that resurrection and reincarnation weren't the same thing? Why do people get their knickers in a twist when all they have to do is spell stuff out in easy to understand language?
Leader	Lord of all life, help us to work together for that day when your kingdom comes and justice and mercy will be seen in all the earth.
Teen	Like when my dad gets to pay for what he's done and the girls who beat me up get found out and . . .
Leader	Look with favour on your people, gather us in your loving arms . . .
Teen	Me too, Lord? Or just them? The regulars? The ones who understand every last word of what's going on?
Leader	And bring us with all the saints to feast at your table in heaven.
Teen	See – I knew it. You have to be a saint to go to heaven. So that's me out.
	They're singing again – and there's a couple of girls and a guy in the choir who are my kind of age. I wish I could . . . like that's ever going to happen.
Leader	Spirit, we worship you, everlasting and almighty:
Congregation	*Spirit, we worship you, everlasting and almighty.*
Teen	OMG, the woman next to me just said I had a lovely voice.
Leader	Through Christ, and with Christ, and in Christ, in the unity of the Holy Spirit, all honour and glory are yours, O loving Father, for ever and ever. Amen.
	Holy God, we worship you, everlasting and almighty:

Congregation *Holy God, we worship you, everlasting and almighty.*

Teen I was going to go but now maybe . . .

Leader As our Saviour has taught us, so we pray.

Congregation *Our Father . . .*

Teen Does that really mean me too?

Congregation *who art in heaven . . .*

Teen I still don't know where that is.

Congregation *hallowed be thy name . . .*

Teen And I'm sorry for all the times I swear and say things like 'Bloody Hell' and 'For Christ's sake . . .'

Congregation *Thy kingdom come; thy will be done, on earth as it is in heaven . . .*

Teen Surely what your will is must be something different from what me and Mandy get at home? I mean, you're gentle Jesus, right? So hitting and punching and all the other stuff – that's not your will, is it? So why don't you do something and stop it? Like now.

Congregation *Give us this day our daily bread . . .*

Teen So they all pray this every week and still there are people starving? How does that work then? And by the way, God, the odd proper meal in our house would be nice.

Congregation *And forgive us our trespasses . . .*

Teen I am sorry. Really. I will try . . . only it's so hard.

Congregation *As we forgive those who trespass against us . . .*

Teen I *can't* forgive him . . . I mean, OK, so the drinking maybe, because I've got hammered a few times so I can't talk but the other stuff . . . no way, God. No way.

Congregation *And lead us not into temptation . . .*

Teen When I go into shops, stop me reaching out and nicking stuff. Please. I don't want to be bad. I really don't.

Congregation *But deliver us from evil . . .*

Teen   Please.

Congregation   *For thine is the kingdom, the power and the glory, for ever and ever. Amen.*

Leader   Jesus is the Lamb of God who takes away the sins of the world. Happy are those who are called to his supper.

Congregation   *Lord, I am not worthy to receive you, but only say the word and I shall be healed.*

Teen   Is it really that easy? One word from you – but what am I doing? I'm talking like you're really there, like you really care . . . but then, all these people must believe you are and you do, and what if they're right, and I'm wrong and there really is a chance that I could . . .

Leader   Draw near with faith. Receive the body of our Lord Jesus Christ which he gave for you, and his blood which he shed for you. Eat and drink in remembrance that he died for you, and feed on him in your hearts by faith with thanksgiving.

Teen   Now they're all filing up and . . . what?
The woman next to me says I can go up too – for a blessing. I don't know – I mean, it doesn't seem right, somehow. It's not like I'm one of them and what if the vicar says get lost? Maybe you have to come every week to qualify. Oh . . . she's standing back to let me through, smiling and nodding like she knows me. I suppose it can't do any harm. I feel a right idiot though. I don't know what to do. It says on this sheet that I just keep my head bowed . . . I don't know.

Hymns during the giving of Communion

I'm accepted, I'm forgiven
Among us and before us
Be still, for the presence of the Lord

After Communion

Teen The vicar guy stopped when he got to me. I nearly died. I thought he was going to tell me I had no right being there. But he didn't. He actually stooped down and touched my shoulder and eyeballed me and then smiled and said something about God keeping me and blessing me and holding me in love. And on my way back to my seat, that fit guy in the choir smiled at me. Like it was totally normal for me to be here.

Leader Father of all, we give you thanks and praise, that when we were still far off . . .

Teen That's how I feel – far off. My world is so far off the way this lot live and as for God, well he's a million miles away. Except that somehow I don't feel as bad as when I came through the door – partly because Dad hasn't found me but . . .

Leader you met us . . .

Teen . . . I've been talking to him – well to myself, and yet . . .

Leader and brought us home.

Teen kept me safe *from* home for a bit, more like, but still . . .

Leader Dying and living, he declared your love . . .

Teen Could you really, truly love me, God? If you do exist . . .

Leader gave us grace . . .

Teen I am *so* not graceful. My nan said I had two left feet.

Leader and opened the gate of glory.
  May we who share Christ's body, live his risen life . . .

Teen Now it's all about the club members again, the ones who ate the bread. And I was just beginning to think . . .

Leader we who drink his cup bring life to others; we whom the Spirit lights . . .

Teen	See? We're back to the 'aren't we wonderful – we've got it sussed' stuff again. And that's making me feel angry and I thought the anger was going away a bit and . . .
Leader	give light to the world . . .
Teen	They could start with me. They could let me join the choir – as if!
Leader	Keep us firm in the hope you have set before us, so we and all your children shall be free . . .
Teen	Free from people sneering at me, free from being tied to looking after Mum and Mandy, free to say how I really feel, free to find someone, somewhere who will love me for me . . .
Leader	and the whole earth live to praise your name.
Teen	If you could do just one of those things, I would come back next Sunday and the Sunday after . . .
Congregation	*Amen.*
Teen	Amen. Amen. Amen. Please. Amen.

Free open prayer

Hymn

Lord, the light of your love (*Shine, Jesus, shine*) *or*
Jesus Christ is waiting

Blessing and dismissal

8

Come and see

A service for Advent

Introduction

There has never been an easier time in history for the spreading of news. Something exciting happens to you? Within minutes you can tell all of your 678 Facebook friends about it, text your relatives in Australia or America, send a photo of the event winging its way around the globe and pop a quick video on YouTube. And – if you are like me – if you haven't had at least a dozen responses within the next hour, you'll be feeling disappointed.

Never has there been an easier time to say 'Come and see'.

But how often do we use this ease of communication to talk openly about what God is doing in our lives? Oh, it's easy enough to send a worship video to a fellow Christian or church leader, or to share an inspirational quote on Facebook (as long, of course, as it's not *too* religious) but what about talking to our more cynical friends, our atheist relatives or – probably more challenging than any – people who have fallen out with God when really it has been their experience of church that's gone awry?

Today we will reflect on two people for whom the words 'Come and see' were life-changing. And as we do so, let's not fall into the trap of thinking that it was easy for them because Jesus was living and working and walking among them. Instead let's remember that when we say 'Come and see', the very first place our friends may catch a glimpse of our Lord is in the way we live, the words we speak and the gentleness with which we share their life journey.

Hymn

Brother, sister, let me serve you

Reading

John 1:43-51

Reflection of Nathaniel

I knew Philip well – well enough to know that he was a cup-half-full type of guy, always excited, always sure that tomorrow was going to be even better than today. Of course, he was young; whereas I'd lived long enough to know that tomorrow rarely lives up to its promise.

OK, I guess that over the years I'd become a bit of a cynic.

So that morning when Philip came rushing up to me as I sat study-ing the Scriptures, I was irritated. I don't like being interrupted when I'm contemplating serious questions and most people respect that. Not Philip. He had barely greeted me before he was off in full flood.

'We've found him, we've found him,' he cried.

I waved my hand at him, gesturing to him that I was busy but he took no notice.

'Hear me out,' he said. 'We've found the One Moses wrote about in the law, the one the prophets talked of.'

I stared at him in disbelief. How long had we been yearning for God to send a messiah to lead Israel into a new age? And how many times had we listened to wandering preachers and prophets declaring that the Messiah was indeed coming, only to find years on that we were still a nation at the mercy of the Romans? And now here was Philip, grinning from ear to ear, and saying the promised One had come and what's more, he'd seen him.

He must have read my expression of derision because he put his hands on my shoulders and looked me straight in the eye.

'It's true,' he insisted. 'It's Jesus – you know, Joseph's son? From Nazareth?'

Well, that did it. I know my Scriptures and I knew full well that there was no prophecy linking the Messiah with the insignificant town of Nazareth. It's the kind of place you visit once and never bother going back to. Philip was still beaming at me so I told him straight.

'Nazareth?' I said. 'Come off it, can anything good come out of that place?' I'm not sure whether I actually spat on the ground but I just wanted Philip to stop his babbling and leave me in peace.

Like that was going to happen.

'Come and see.' That's what he said. No argument, no backchat – he just smiled and repeated the words.

'Come and see.'

My heart missed a beat. Just hours before I had been reading the words of the psalmist. 'Come and see what God has done.' I had prayed that God would manifest his purpose for me, for Israel . . . and now those words were being spoken directly to me by a young man stretching out his hand to show me the way.

So I went with him.

Hymn

Will you come and follow me?

Nathaniel

I will never forget those first words that Jesus spoke to me. Of course, since then we have conversed many, many times, but that day he said two things that blew my mind. As I walked towards him, he smiled and stepped forward to greet me.

'Here is a true man of Israel,' he said. 'A man without a trace of deceit or pretence in him!'

I didn't get it. I'd never seen this man before and there he was pretending to know all about me. I asked him straight – how did he know who I was? Or what kind of man I was for that matter?

He looked deep into my eyes and he said, 'Before Philip called you, when you were under the fig tree, I saw you.'

And you know what? To this day, I'm not sure what hit me first – the look of pure delight and love in his eyes, or the words he spoke. I felt my heart lift in a way that words cannot describe. And I knew, I just knew beyond any shadow of doubt, that this was the Messiah, the long-awaited, yearned-for Saviour of Israel.

You might ask why – why would something like that happen in a fraction of a second? When we Jews speak of being under the fig tree, it is our way of saying we are studying the Word of God. Jesus couldn't have seen me reading when Philip came to me; I was completely hidden from view. But this man could see; because I knew he could see right into my heart. He saw beyond my intellectual gifts, beyond the years of studying the law and the prophets, beyond the hours of debate and discourse with friends and colleagues. He saw beyond all that to the broken me; to the me who never really felt good enough, never really believed that I deserved the respect that people showed, never really thought that in the great scheme of things, I would amount to anything.

But in Jesus, I saw the one who wasn't bothered about my view of myself, or indeed anyone else's. When he said that I would see greater things than that, that I would see heaven opened and the angels of God ascending and descending on the Son of Man, I didn't know what lay ahead; but as I remembered the story of Jacob's dream I knew this man, this Jesus, would open heaven for me and for everyone who came to him.

I never left him after that. I knew that in following him I would find the peace I yearned for. What I didn't realise back then was that a stark wooden cross would be his Jacob's ladder.

Silence

Hymn

We have a gospel to proclaim

Reading

Mark 7:31-37

Reflection of the deaf mute

I had never had many friends. Just two in fact: Joshua and Jacob. But in the end, that proved to be enough.

I was born deaf and I never learned to speak. Most people don't know how to handle folk like me – after all, they can't have a conversation with me and even though I reckon I'm pretty good at miming and gesturing, they soon lose patience and find better things to do. I probably come across as a bit dim – I'm not, but it's hard when you can't keep up with the current gossip, when you can't hear cartwheels rattling up behind you or pick up the warning mutterings before someone hurls a stone your way. If people are patient I can lip-read; trouble is most people aren't.

Most people, that is, apart from Joshua and Jacob. When they came running up to my shack early one morning, gesturing to me to come with them, I was only half awake. I shook my head, grinned and gestured to the sun which was only just above the horizon. I yawned expecting them to laugh and say they'd come back later.

But they didn't. Joshua squatted down in front of me and mouthed, 'You have to come to see the man Jesus. He will make you well.'

He had to mouth it three times, not because I couldn't lip-read but because I thought he had gone crazy. What man Jesus? And did he really think anyone could restore my hearing and my speech? I glanced up at Jacob, but he was nodding furiously, tapping his foot and beckoning to me to get a move on. In the end he grabbed my wrist and began tugging so I thought – what the heck? It's not as though my life has a great deal of excitement in it and if they wanted to take me to see some fake healer guy, I might as well humour them.

So I went.

Hymn

When Jesus the healer passed through Galilee

Deaf mute

The crowd was massive. Of course, I couldn't hear a sound but as I scanned their faces I could see that they were all silent, not a single mouth moving. That's when Joshua pointed to the man standing on a rock.

'Jesus,' he mouthed. 'Jesus.'

Then he dragged me through the crowd, pushing and shoving people out of the way with his elbows, with Jacob hot on our heels. Judging by the expressions on some of their faces, it was just as well I couldn't hear the expletives they were undoubtedly hurling at my friends.

They reached the front of the crowd just as the man Jesus had stopped speaking and was turning away. Jacob ran up to him and tugged on his sleeve. He was too far away for me to lip-read but within seconds, Jesus had turned and was looking directly at me. He nodded gently and Joshua shoved me forward.

I was so embarrassed; don't get me wrong, my friends were doing their best, but I knew it was hopeless. I gestured to Jesus that, honestly, he didn't need to bother; I realised there was no hope.

You know what? He just smiled, took my arm and led me aside, away from the crowd, behind a couple of olive trees. And then he stuck his fingers in my ears. Everything started spinning; I heard – yes I heard – a humming in my head as if a dozen fruit flies were doing battle with one another. And before I could draw breath, Jesus spat onto his finger, raised his eyes heavenwards, mouthed something at the sky and then touched my tongue, the spittle still on his finger.

'What are you doing?' I had pulled back from him before I realised. I had spoken the words out loud! People came running – Joshua and Jacob in the lead, broad grins on their faces. The crowd began babbling in astonishment.

'You are healed,' Jesus said. And I heard him. My whole body shook, tears poured down my face, but I didn't care. I dropped to my knees, touching his feet, my shoulders shaking.

Gently he raised me to my feet.

'Do not tell anyone about this,' he said, his gaze moving from my face to the crowd around me.

Well, did he really expect anyone to keep quiet about a miracle like that? Least of all me – I had a voice. I could hear – the birds singing, people talking, the sound of my own sandals slapping on the ground as I ran to Joshua and Jacob and hugged them.

Don't tell anyone? I wanted the whole world to know what this miracle maker had done for me. So I took no notice of what he said: I told anyone who would listen and the crowd that followed him got bigger and bigger.

It wasn't until a few weeks later, having followed him around wherever he went, that I realised why he wanted us all to keep quiet. He performed miracles – but he did so much more. When he spoke, his words opened our hearts and our minds in the same way he had opened my ears and restored my voice. He talked of a new way to live, of a kingdom where what you looked like, what you could do, how much money you had would mean nothing. Some of the people who came to him wanted a quick fix; to be healed and carry on living as they always had.

It doesn't work that way. Once you have been with Jesus for any length of time, you can't be who you were. It just isn't possible.

Silence

Hymn

Lord, for the years *or* Blessed assurance *or* I've found a friend

Prayers of intercession

Lord Jesus Christ, they came to you – the blind, the deaf, the mute, those who could not walk, those whose minds were troubled – and you healed them. And in the healing, they were changed. Lord, heal us – heal us of our jealousies, our anger, our bitterness, our unbelief. Touch us where we hurt and anoint us with the balm of your under-standing and your peace. Then Lord, send us out with the courage and the determination to spread your Word and to live in your light, wherever and however you ask us. Amen.

(Here follow intercessory prayers for the congregation, community and wider world.)

Hymn

I, the Lord of sea and sky

Blessing and dismissal

9

Expect the unexpected

A service for the Christmas Season

Introduction

Christmas can be a very dangerous time. In the run-up to the festive season, our newspapers are full of dire warnings, some very sensible: 'don't drink and drive'; 'do make sure the juices run clear before you eat your turkey'; 'extinguish all candles before going to bed.' Others possibly less so, such as the numerous column inches devoted to the health and safety risks of Christmas: paper cuts caused by over-eager unwrapping of presents or the risks of pine needles in the toes if decorating the tree barefoot.

But one warning seems conspicuous by its absence. *Don't over-sentimentalise the Christmas story.* It's so easy to do: designers of Christmas cards revel in the spotlessly-robed Virgin, the docile cattle, the manger overflowing with fresh hay. It's all very pretty; it's all very heart-warming. And it's all a dumbed-down version of how it must have been.

God chose ordinary people for the most extraordinary task: the raising of his Son, the longed-for Messiah. He chose the lowest of the low to be the first to see the Saviour and the most humble of dwellings for his birth. But these events didn't take place in isolation; for every character featured in our Nativity plays or depicted on our Christmas cards, there were dozens of others: ordinary people going about their ordinary everyday business, people on the edge, not only of society, but of the events that would change the world for ever. And for the central characters – Mary and Joseph – the fact that they were chosen by God didn't mean that the pain of labour, the worry about earning a living, the fear of rejection by family and friends wasn't as real and as ongoing as it is for us today.

When we over-sentimentalise the Nativity story, we run the risk of dumbing-down the mystery and the wonder – and the reassurance – of knowing that God was made man and knew in the most minute detail just what it means to be human.

Hymn

Love came down at Christmas

Reflection of Joseph

We lost Jesus last week. Not just for an hour or so – that's happened many times before, because he was always the type of kid who wandered off when something in the distance caught his interest. No, this time it was for three days. We were journeying home from Jerusalem after the Passover – I thought Jesus was with Mary, and she thought he was with me. It wasn't until we pitched camp for the night that we realised he was missing. None of his friends had seen him; and that was unusual because he was always hanging out with one lad or another.

We set off back towards the city, retracing our steps, calling his name – but nothing. Mary was distraught – terrified that something dreadful had happened to him. Of course I kept telling her not to worry, reassuring her that we would find him. But as time went by and there was still no sign of him, real fear gripped my heart.

I couldn't sleep that second night. All I could think about was how it had all begun – and the more I remembered the events of 12 years earlier, the more the fear overwhelmed me. The fear that I had now done what I had always dreaded doing.

I had failed God. I had failed to keep his Son safe.

Reading

Matthew 1:18-23

Joseph

I will never forget the day that Mary came home; the day when my world changed forever.

I was on the roof of Simon's house, putting the finishing touches to the fresh plaster, when I saw it – a cloud of dust being thrown up by the wheels of a cart. I straightened and shaded my eyes from the sun – and my heart missed a beat. It was her – Mary, my darling, adorable wife-to-be – home at last! How I had missed her all those weeks she had been with her cousin Elizabeth. I had spent all my free moments working on the house we would live in together, and I couldn't wait to show her what I'd done. I watched as the cart pulled up outside the home of Leah and Samuel, her cousins who had cared for her since her parents' death; I smiled as the neighbours rushed out to greet her. She has always been popular, my Mary – and it wasn't more than a couple of seconds before she was surrounded. My heart swelled with pride, and I bent to smooth the last bit of plaster, eager to get down there and greet her.

That's when it happened. Little Abigail, Simon's granddaughter, ran over to Mary, calling her name; Mary bent down to hug her and a gust of wind caught the fringe of her shawl, and blew it to the ground.

And all the cries of welcome and eager shouts stopped in an instant. For a moment, no one moved. Mary stood motionless. Then, from somewhere in the throng a woman's voice cried, 'No!'

I peered down to see what had caused the commotion. And my world came crashing down.

The curve of her stomach, plain to see as the wind caught her dress and blew it back. Everything within in me shrieked, 'No'! I was being stupid – it was just a slight increase in her weight, after all Elizabeth, she had often told me, kept a good table. And perhaps she hadn't worked as hard with her cousin as she did at home. But then, as the mutterings of the crowd grew louder, I saw her slowly but firmly place both hands protectively on her stomach.

And with that gesture, I knew. Mary was with child. And it wasn't mine.

Reading

Psalm 34:7-9

Silence

Prayer

Lord our God, in our moments of frenzied fear or red hot anger, we are at our most vulnerable. We lash out – at others, at ourselves, at you. We judge everything by the standards of the world, we see everything in black and white, and we want everything to be the way we believe it should be. In these moments, Father, still us: hold us: calm us. And then speak to us of your vision, your truth, and your plan for us. Thank you that you understand our outbursts, our fears and our disbelief; thank you that you can take everything we throw at you and transform it into the beginnings of an even deeper, more wonderful relationship. Amen.

Hymn

Dear Lord and Father of mankind *or* Make me a channel of your peace

Reflection of Simon

I had decided to come back to the house early; I wanted to see how Joseph was getting on with the plastering. To be honest, I was impatient for it to be finished: my wife had been nagging and Joseph – well, he'd been distracted recently. I knew he was busy on his own house, getting it ready for his marriage to Mary but no way did I want that to get in the way of him finishing the job for me. What's more, I'd spotted Mary arriving back home and didn't want him downing tools and dashing off to welcome her. He wouldn't do that if I had anything to do with it.

I had just rounded the corner when I saw him. He was belting along the road, sandals flapping – and he was running in the opposite direction from Mary's house. Well, that got me worried, I can tell you. Had he botched the job of my plastering, seen me coming and made a run for it? No, I knew that was ridiculous; Joseph was a meticulous craftsman and a totally honest man; if there was a problem, he would hold his hands up and admit to it. So what on earth had happened?

Hymn

Let me have my way among you (*Do not strive*) *or* Soften my heart

Reflection of Joseph

All I remember was that I ran and ran, away from Simon's house, away from the village, up into the hills, stumbling on the rocky path, until the stitch in my side vied with the pain in my heart. Finally I could run no more, and I veered off the path into an olive grove and sank to the ground, beating my fists against my head and yes – I confess – crying like a kid. I wanted to be sick; I wanted to hit someone; I wanted to grab hold of Mary and shake her and make her tell me what she had been thinking of.

But despite all that anger and grief, something inside me told me that Mary couldn't have, wouldn't have, betrayed me. A thousand images began tumbling through my head. Did she meet some opportunist lout while she was away? But surely Elizabeth and Zechariah would have kept her close to them and besides, no Jewish boy known to such a priestly family would dare . . . oh, dear God! The Romans! Had one of them done this to her? Had she been raped?

However it had happened, one thing was clear: I had to divorce her. No self-respecting Jew with a reputation and a business to protect could be seen to have any dealings with a woman who allowed herself to be used like that. But what if it wasn't her fault? What if . . . ?

No matter. Whatever the circumstances, I knew she was soiled goods. Tarnished. Trash. I had no choice but to get rid of her; one thing was certain, my business would suffer if I was seen to hesitate, to even think of associating for one day more with a girl who was no longer a virgin.

I began scrambling to my feet, intent on heading back in the direction of Nazareth, but the nausea gripped at my throat and the ground appeared to rise up before and spin in front of my eyes. I sank down, cursing myself for running so far and so fast in the heat. I closed my eyes; perhaps it was better if I just rested a bit. Better for me – and for Mary. I would wait – wait until it was dark. I couldn't, wouldn't, add to the family's shame; if I could just do what had to be done quietly and with dignity, suggest perhaps that she went back to Elizabeth until the fuss had died down, then maybe she wouldn't have to face the abuse and the rejection. Despite my hurt and my pain, I couldn't bear to think of her chased out of the village, stoned, killed even . . . not my Mary, my precious Mary.

But, of course, she wasn't my Mary any longer.

As the dizziness took hold, I closed my eyes and tried to blot out the image of Mary standing in the street, her shame visible for all to see. But all I felt was a pain in my heart like nothing I had ever felt before.

Hymn

God moves in a mysterious way *or* Be bold, be strong

(*During this section of the reflection the words of the angel are spoken by another character who can be out of sight of the congregation or visible.*)

Joseph My eyes were heavy with sleep when I sensed someone dropping to the ground beside me and laying a hand on my shoulder. I tried to focus but the sinking sun was shining directly into my eyes. Try as I would I couldn't open my eyes wide enough to see who was there.

Angel Joseph, Joseph, you're a descendant of David, right? So put all thoughts of denouncing and divorcing Mary out of your mind right now! The baby she is carrying isn't the result of anything bad or immoral that's happened to her.

Joseph I forced my eyes open, trying to frame words in my head but it seemed my lips wouldn't move. The man beside me seemed to be shimmering in a heat haze; in fact he didn't really resemble any of the men from around Nazareth.

Angel Mary has done nothing wrong. The child she is carrying has been conceived by God's Holy Spirit. It is God's Son she is carrying.

Joseph Again I opened my mouth but couldn't utter a single word.

Angel Mary will have a little boy and you have been chosen by God to be his earthly father. You will call him Jesus because he will be the one who saves people; saves them from all their wrongdoing and misguided ways and sinful behaviour.

Joseph By now the guy was leaning so close to me that I could feel his breath on my cheek, drying the moisture of my tears. I wanted to shout and tell him he was an idiot but then he said something that made my heart miss a beat.

Angel All this is happening so that what the prophets said might be brought to fruition: A virgin will be pregnant and bear a son and they shall call his name Emmanuel, which means 'God with us.' You do remember?

Joseph   Well, of course I did – what Jewish guy whose parents brought him up in the faith wouldn't remember the prophecy about the Messiah who would save them. But here? Now? And . . . me? Us?

  The man touched my arm and my flesh tingled.

Angel   God is with you, Joseph. He has chosen you, just as he has chosen Mary. So put away your fears, ignore the gossips and do as God wants. It's OK. Don't be afraid.

Joseph   Don't be afraid? What was the man on? 'Hang on!' I shouted, relief pouring over me as I realised I could suddenly speak. I sat bolt upright and looked around. He had gone. And the ground where he had been sitting bore no imprint. The grass was as straight as it had always been.

Hymn

Father, I place into your hands *or* I do not know what lies ahead

Joseph   I went at once to Mary's house, keeping my eyes straight ahead, ignoring the whispers and pitying glances of the village women who, despite the lateness of the hour, still seemed to be finding reasons to be sweeping the road in front of their houses. As I knocked on the door, bursting in without waiting for a reply, three pairs of eyes met mine. Samuel had the look of a man struggling to contain his anger; his wife was pale and trembling. But it was the look in Mary's piercing blue eyes that will stay with me forever. It was a look that said 'Please believe me.'

  'You have come to annul the betrothal,' Samuel grunted.

  'I have come,' I replied, 'to set the date for my wedding to Mary.'

  One look at Mary's face and I knew. I knew I was doing the right thing. I knew this was out of my hands and from now on, I would have to trust in God as I had never trusted before.

Silence

Hymn

Guide me, O thou great Jehovah *or* Take my life and let it be

Prayer

Father God, to do what is right is often not easy, it is not what comes most naturally, and it is not something that makes us comfortable or relaxed. When we face criticism or ridicule for taking a stand which goes against the culture or perception of those around us, we pray that you would draw really close to us, because without you, we know we will stumble and fall, back off, compromise or simply give in. Make your presence felt, Lord, in our hearts, in our silences, in our moments of cowardice and in our moments of stepping out; and may your light shine through the cracks of our flawed natures and point to a better way to be, to act and to love. Amen.

Reflection of Joseph

All that happened nearly 13 years ago – and every morning since, my first words on opening my eyes have been 'God my Father, show me the way.' It hasn't been easy – in fact, the first three years were just one big struggle, one challenge after another. But gradually, life took on a more normal pattern and Jesus grew to be a cheerful, fun-loving but very thoughtful boy. I adored him and I don't think I'm exaggerating when I say that I was pretty special to him too. I never forgot, of course, who was his real father – but I admit that, with every passing year, I felt more and more like any other dad in the village.

Until last week. We found him, our lost son, sitting in the Temple listening to the rabbis – and you know what? He was so engrossed in their words that he didn't even see us coming. Mary did what all mums do – burst into tears of relief, rapidly followed by shouting at Jesus and asking him what on earth he thought he was doing, causing us so much worry.

Even if I live to be a very old man, I don't think I will ever forget his response.

'But surely, you must have known I would be here in my Father's house?'

And while the teachers clustered around us, telling us how amazing Jesus was, what incredible perception and understanding he showed for one so young, those words kept ringing in my ears.

'You must have known I would be here in my Father's house.'

Of course, we have known – Mary and I – that Jesus has a destiny way beyond our understanding, that Jesus is God's own Son. We had begun to explain to him the circumstances surrounding his birth. But that day in the Temple, I realised that he already knew, and felt, and acknowledged, that his father was and always would be God. He is ours on loan only – but then, I guess all children are gifts from God, entrusted to our care until they leave to fulfil their own destiny.

Knowing it doesn't make it any easier. But all I can do is trust in God, his Father. God trusted me – and I guess he will go on trusting me to do what is needed and to let go when the time comes.

I pray I will never fail him.

Prayers of intercession

Lord Jesus Christ, so often we lose you too. The demands of our day-to-day lives, the pressures to earn money, pay bills, nurture our families, play our part in the community and keep pace with an ever more rapidly changing world, can occupy every waking moment. And suddenly, we feel the gap in our lives, and turn to you – only to feel as if you are no longer there. But Lord, you are there; waiting for us to walk that extra mile to find you. Help us always to keep space in every day to come to you, and yes, if necessary to cry with you, shout at you, plead with you – because you can take it. Remind us, Lord, that it is not our erratic emotions that distress you but our absence, that in coming to you our healing has already begun. Amen.

(*Here follow intercessory prayers for the congregation, community and wider world.*)

Hymn

Put all your trust in God *or* Father, hear the prayer we offer

Blessing and dismissal

10

Scruffy children sketch

A children's service for Christmas Eve

Preparation

This sketch can be used as part of a children's or family service on Christmas Eve or Christmas morning. The 'characters' used in this story should be adults or older teens dressed as children (St Trinian's style).

Characters

The Very Scruffy Girl; The Exceedingly Messy Boy; The Bossy Boy; The Very Prim, Stuck-Up Girl; various other boys and girls; Minister

Minister   Welcome everyone, to our Christmas Eve service. Tomorrow, as you all know, is Christmas Day. And whose birthday are we celebrating? That's right – it will be Jesus' birthday.

Stand to sing carol to the tune of 'Sing a song of sixpence'.

Sing a song of Christmas, a baby in the hay,
sing a song for Jesus, born on Christmas Day,
sing a song of shepherds, angels said to them
go and see the Saviour who is born in Bethlehem.
Sing a song of wise men following a star,
bringing gifts to Jesus travelling so far,
sing a song for Jesus lying in the hay
born to make us happy, born for us on Christmas Day.

Sit; light candles; sing 'Happy Birthday' to Jesus.

Minister   Now I want to tell you the story of Christmas. So are you sitting comfortably? Then I'll . . . good gracious, what on earth is happening?

The door swings open and a group of noisy, messy children thunder in.

Prim Girl See, – we're late! I told you we'd be late (*punches Messy Boy*). It's all your fault!

Messy Boy (*hopefully*) So can we go home, then?

Prim Girl (*disdainfully*) No, we can't go home.

Messy Boy Why not? There's nowhere to sit.

Scruffy Girl And I want to watch a DVD! (*or 'play with my new toys' if it's Christmas morning*)

Prim Girl Well, you can't! We can't go home because it's Christmas. Everyone goes to church at Christmas. It's the rules.

Scruffy Girl Why?

Prim Girl Don't you know *anything*? Because Jesus got born at Christmas.

Scruffy Girl (*puzzled*) I got born on June the third, but we don't go to church because of that.

Prim Girl (*scornfully*) That's because *you* aren't important. Jesus *was* important. He made a difference to everyone's life. (*turns to Minister in a sucking up, simpering sort of way*) That's right, isn't it?

Minister It is.

Bossy Boy (*woefully*) Our baby made a difference to our lives. Now we don't get any sleep and there's always sick on the carpet.

Minister Look, it's standing room only here. There's no room for a load of noisy kids who . . . Hang on, haven't I heard that line somewhere before? Well, I do need some volunteers to help me tell the story. Would you four like to volunteer? If you want to stay, that is?

All four look sheepish.

Bossy Boy OK, let's go for it.

Minister Good. Just stay there and join in the next carol.

Carol

Come and join the celebration

All sit.

Minister	Let's start the story at the beginning. The Emperor Caesar ordered that everyone had to make a journey back to where they were born to be registered.
Prim Girl	Like the register at school?
Minister	Something like that, yes. Joseph and Mary went to be registered. Mary was expecting a baby . . .
Scruffy Girl	She must have been really fed up having to go walk-about at a time like that.
Minister	(*thoughtfully*) I suppose she might have been. Anyway, off they went, sometimes riding on a donkey, sometimes walking. It was a very, very long way. Now, I need two people to play Mary and Joseph.
Scruffy Girl	I'll be Mary!
Prim Girl	*You? You?* You can't be Mary. Mary wore long robes and smiled all the time. She was kind of pure and stuff. You're dirty and you frown a lot. (*leans towards her*) And you smell! Mary couldn't have been like that!
Scruffy Girl	She would have been too! She (*pointing at Minister*) said they went on a donkey, or walked. So she'd have been hot and sweaty – and grumpy, what with the baby kicking her in the ribs and everything.
Minister	You've got a point. OK, you can be Mary.
Prim Girl	Huh!
Scruffy Girl	(*pointing to Messy Boy*) And he can be Joseph. He's my boyfriend. We're in love.

Minister   Very well.

They hold hands.

Minister   So – Mary and Joseph journeyed on until they reached Bethlehem. And then it was time for Mary to have her baby . . .

Scruffy Girl   (*clutches her stomach*) Ow! Ouch! Oooooh!

Minister   What on earth's the matter?

Scruffy Girl   You said she had her baby. I'm having it.

Minister   Ah. Well, wait a minute, could you? Joseph was very worried when he realised that Mary was soon to give birth and he stopped at an inn and asked for a room. (*Minister pauses*) So now we need an innkeeper.

Bossy Boy   (*jumps up*) I'll be him.

Minister   The innkeeper told Joseph that the place was full up.

Bossy Boy   (*in role of innkeeper*) Sorry mate, we're chockablock here. Not an inch of space left.

Joseph   But the baby's coming. We have to find a room. You have to help us.

Innkeeper   It'd be more than my job's worth to let anyone else in.

Minister   (*in a stage whisper*) Offer him the stable.

Innkeeper   What d'ya say?

Minister   The innkeeper told Joseph that he and Mary could sleep in the stable.

Innkeeper   He did?

Minister   (*losing patience slightly*) Yes, he did. So do it please.

Innkeeper   (*shrugging*) You can have the stable if you like. But don't expect room service because . . .

Minister   Thank you – that's fine. So Mary and Joseph went to the stable.

Scruffy Girl (*sobs and clutches Joseph's arm*) Boo hoo!

Minister What's the matter now?

Scruffy Girl I'm scared. Well, she would have been, wouldn't she? She hasn't had a kid before – and she's miles from home, and no one's being very welcoming, are they?

Prim Girl But Mary was holy. So she wouldn't have cried.

Scruffy Girl Get real. She would too.

Messy Boy What would Joseph have done?

Scruffy Girl Walked up and down and gone out for a fag.

Minister Thank you – that will do. Then, after a few hours, the baby was born. And Mary wrapped him in swaddling cloths.

Bossy Boy In what?

Minister Tightly wrapped blankets to make him feel safe. And she put him in a manger.

Bossy Boy Our baby had a cot.

Minister But Jesus had a manger – the trough that held the straw and hay for the cows to eat.

Prim Girl Poor little thing. Didn't Social Services make them give him a cot?

Minister They didn't have Social Services then. They had to go it alone. Now for the next part of the story I need shepherds. And an angel.

Scruffy Girl I'll be the angel as well . . .

Prim Girl She's no angel – my mother says . . .

Minister That's enough. *You* (*to Prim Girl*) can be the Angel of the Lord.

Prim Girl What do I have to do?

Minister Just listen. And you (*to Bossy Boy*) can be a shepherd.

Bossy Boy But I haven't got any sheep.

Minister   You'll just have to imagine the sheep.

Bossy Boy   (*pointing to kids in the congregation*) Then you'll have to be lambs. Go 'Baa'.

Minister   Now there were shepherds on the hillside keeping watch over their sheep. (*kids in congregation bleat*) And there was suddenly a bright light and an angel appeared in the sky. The shepherds were afraid.

Bossy Boy   I'm not afraid of anything, me.

Minister   You're a shepherd. You're afraid. OK?

Bossy Boy starts to shake and tremble in an exaggerated manner.

Minister   And then the angel spoke to them and said

Angel   (*butting in and speaking loudly*) Hey, you shepherd! Don't be afraid! I've got this mega-amazing news. There's this baby and he's special. You'll find him wrapped in swaddling cloths and lying in a trough.

Scruffy Girl   Manger!

Angel   Same thing.

Minister   And then a huge crowd of angels appeared in the sky, praising God and singing – and this is where we all get to be angels . . .

The congregation sings the Peruvian Gloria.

Minister   And then the angels disappeared.

Scruffy Girl   (*shoving angel*) So disappear!

Minister   So the shepherds went quickly and found the stable.

The shepherds move over to where Mary and Joseph are.

At this point Mary picks up the baby Jesus, tips him over her shoulder and burps him.

Prim Girl   What are you doing?

Mary	Burping Jesus.
Prim Girl	You can't do that! Jesus is holy. This is a church. You can't go around burping baby Jesus.
Mary	Why not? He's a baby, isn't he? So he burps. Babies do. They can't help it. *(she sniffs his bottom)*. And they pooh. And they cry.
Minister	Of course he did. Jesus came to earth as part of a human family. That was the miracle of Christmas. If he hadn't been like you and me, from the very beginning, he couldn't have done all the things he did for us.
Messy Boy	So did he have tantrums?
Bossy Boy	And throw his food on the floor?
Messy Boy	And throw up on his mother's clothes when she was going out?
Minister	I'm sure he did. So – that is the story of Christmas.
Prim Girl	Hang on! Hang on! You've missed a bit.
Minister	I have?
Prim Girl	The Three Kings and the presents.
The Others	Presents? What presents?
Prim Girl	The Three Kings brought presents, right? Gold, frankincense and myrrh.
Minister	They did – but not till later. On Christmas night it was just ordinary people who came to see Jesus. Not the rich and famous, or the powerful or the clever, but just a few shepherds.
Scruffy Girl	. . . and probably the innkeeper and his wife and the other guests.
Messy Boy	And maybe some kids who were hanging around.
Prim Girl	Kids didn't hang around in the Bible.
Scruffy Girl	I bet they did. Cos there wasn't any telly to watch, was there?
Bossy Boy	I wish I'd been there.

Prim Girl	Me too.
Minister	Well, in a way, you are there. Because you're here, celebrating the day that Jesus was born. And that's the real magic of the Christmas story. Jesus is here, for us, today, tomorrow, always. (*looks at children*) And that's the best present of all. Happy Christmas.
All	Happy Christmas!

Carol

Away in a manger

Prayer

(*The response after each prayer is 'Hear us, Lord Jesus.'*)

We pray for peace in our homes and throughout the world tonight.

Hear us, Lord Jesus.

We pray for people keeping the peace and keeping public services working while we rest.

Hear us, Lord Jesus.

We pray for people like Mary and Joseph who are in search of food and shelter and for those trying to help them.

Hear us, Lord Jesus.

We pray for the children who will be born tonight and for their families.

Hear us, Lord Jesus.

We pray for all the people who work to build a secure future for young people in need.

Hear us, Lord Jesus.

We bring our prayers together in the words that Jesus taught us:

Our Father who art in heaven,
hallowed be thy name;
thy kingdom come;
thy will be done;
on earth as it is in heaven.
Give us this day our daily bread.
And forgive us our trespasses,
as we forgive those who trespass against us.
And lead us not into temptation,
but deliver us from evil.
For thine is the kingdom,
the power and the glory,
for ever and ever.
Amen.

Carol

O little town of Bethlehem

11

Fear not

A service for Christmas Week

Introduction

This is the week during which thousands of children will wear their dressing gowns in church or school, put tea towels on their heads and tuck toy lambs under their arms. Harassed mothers will fashion angels' wings from coat hangers and the remnants of an old net curtain, and teachers will tell again the story of a windswept hillside outside a town called Bethlehem.

This is also a week during which thousands of people, young and old, will huddle in doorways, crowd into night shelters, avert their eyes from the sight of families cheerfully loading trolleys with vast quantities of food and drink, and try not to look back or forward. A week when the need to find something, anything, that will blot out the hurt and the pain is even stronger and harder to resist than usual. A week when newspapers will run appeals to help the homeless and give a Christmas meal to those who go hungry. For those who receive, this week may be the one that changes their lives.

This week was – and could still be – a life-changing week for anyone who really hears.

Prayer

God our Father, the stories of those who were part of the astonishing events in Bethlehem two thousand years ago are so familiar to us that sometimes we feel there is nothing new to hear. The deprivation, the tragedies and the yearnings of your people in the world today are made so familiar to us through newspapers and television that those too can be absorbed into the fabric of our lives and seen as something inevitable, something beyond our power to change. Today, here, now, Lord, open our ears, our eyes, our hearts and our minds and fill us with the energy that comes when your Spirit moves us to hear the unspoken, to see the hidden and to understand our role in bringing the dark places into your light. Amen.

Carol

While shepherds watched

Reflection of the oldest shepherd

The wife thought I'd finally flipped. She's got a sharp tongue on her at the best of times and she didn't mince her words, I can tell you – called me an old fool and accused me of drinking too much fermented wine. As if I'd have enough money for even a mouthful of the stuff – but then that's Rebekah for you; always got an answer for everything.

I suppose you couldn't blame her. I mean, all these years on, I still can't get my head around it and I was there. Amazing things don't happen to the likes of me and my mates. It's an out of the ordinary day if someone in the village actually looks us in the eye and speaks to us. The lowest of the low, bottom of the social scale, that's us. Which, when you come to think of it, is pretty rich considering we're the ones out there on the hillsides in all weathers, putting our lives at risk to protect the sheep from predators.

And that night was a cold one. It was never so bad for the young chaps – they don't seem to notice the plummeting temperatures; but I'm getting on in years and my bones ache at the best of times – cold and damp just makes them worse. Our small fire gave out scarcely enough heat to keep our hands warm, and the light drizzle didn't help when we tried to fan the flames. I was in a pretty foul mood that night if I'm honest – and I took it out on Asher. He's young enough to be my grandson – a nice enough lad, but a bit of a dreamer, always stargazing and making up stories about the pictures he sees in the sky. Well, he won't have to fantasise any more, that's for sure.

When Asher cried out, leaping to his feet and grabbing my arm, my first thought was that he'd seen a wolf. I seized my staff and shouted to the other men – and then realised that Asher was staring up at the sky. At the same time I realised it was getting light – far too early and far too rapidly. Something was wrong.

And then I saw him.

Hymn

Angels we have heard on high

Reading

Luke 2:8-10

Reflection of the Angel of the Lord

'Do not be afraid.' How often over the centuries have I and those like me uttered those words to frightened mortals! For you cannot get a message over to anyone until they feel safe – and sometimes it takes a while to calm them down – and then you need to repeat yourself over and over to make sure they've understood. It was no different that night – the night when he came, when God our heavenly and most awesome creator took on human form. Not just any human form but that of a tiny, vulnerable and totally dependent baby, which to be honest seemed to us a strange way of going about things when you consider he could have chosen any way he wanted to present himself to humankind. But God has always acted contrary to expectations – even heavenly ones!

What was more extraordinary was that we were to bring this life-changing news to a group of shepherds on a windswept hillside. Of course, the problem with that was that we – well, I, because to start with we reckoned the appearance of all of us in one fell swoop would finish them off! – the problem was that I preferred dealing with humans on a one-to-one basis. Get them in a crowd and fear spreads like wildfire – and that's what I was afraid would happen that night. So I made a plan. I had seen a young boy – quite a lot younger than the rest – gazing at the stars with a look of awe and fascination on his face, and at once I knew he was the one I should appear to first. And I have to say it was a good choice; sure he jumped out of his skin and grabbed the arm of the shepherd sitting next to him, but he didn't back off and he didn't for one moment take his eyes off me.

We had made a connection, and with humans, that's always the right way to start.

Carol

The first Nowell

Reading

Luke 2:11-14

Reflection of the youngest shepherd

At first I thought it was some sort of shooting star. The light was so bright that I was dazzled and had to shield my eyes. But then, as I took my hand away from my face, I saw a figure floating from the centre of the light. And the figure had wings.

'Do not be afraid.' That's what he said.

All around me I could hear the panicked cries of the other men, but the moment the angel uttered those words an inexplicable sense of calm flooded my body. Our eyes met and, despite the howling wind and the raw dampness in the air, my body felt as warm as if I had been sitting by a roaring fire.

'I have come to give you wonderful news,' the angel said.

'Me?' I stammered and you know what? The angel laughed. Actually laughed. I didn't know holy beings giggled but they do.

'For all of you – and for everyone in the world!' he said. He raised an arm and gestured down the hill to the town. 'Tonight, over there in Bethlehem, David's own city, the Saviour, Christ the Lord has been born!'

I felt a hand on my arm.

'Is this for real?' Old Zebulun's voice was even shakier than usual.

The angel smiled down on him.

'You'll know it's for real when you see him! You'll find him wrapped in swaddling clothes and lying in a feeding trough.'

'See him? Who? How?' The murmurs of the others echoed all around me, but I couldn't tear my eyes away from the angel who seemed to be drifting away, higher and higher, into the night sky, his fingers splayed outwards. For a moment it looked as if sparks were flying out of him and then, suddenly, the whole sky lit up and a host of angels flooded my whole field of vision. I don't know how to describe it; all the usual sounds of the night – the bleating of the sheep, the distant howling of a wolf, the trickling of the stream over the nearby rocks – were all blotted out by the joyful calls of the smiling angels.

'Glory to God in the highest and on earth, peace to all on whom his gift of love rests.'

The light grew brighter and brighter until we could bear it no longer and had to hide our faces.

And then, suddenly, there was silence. The skies were empty, with just a few stars twinkling in the black expanse.

Carol

Angels from the realms of glory *or* It came upon the midnight clear (*The Gloria may be sung here as an alternative or addition.*)

Reading

Luke 2:15

Reflection of the oldest shepherd

My mind was in turmoil. I knew that what I'd seen was real because all the others had seen it too. What I couldn't get my head around was the message – that the promised Saviour had actually been born, here, in my home town. I may not be a well-read man but I know as well as any other Jew that the prophet Micah foretold that the Messiah would be born in Bethlehem! That's what decided me: sheep or no sheep, I was going down to the town to see for myself.

There's one advantage of being the oldest: you can pull rank when you have to. Asher was the youngest, but no way was I going to ask him to stay behind with the flock – for one thing, he was such a dreamer that the wolves would have had a field day and, besides, I knew he'd refuse and that would make me look a fool. So I told Timothy and Reuben that they were in charge, and the rest of us headed off before they could protest.

At first we didn't know where to look – after all, there are dozens of outhouses with feeding troughs in a place like Bethlehem, but as we passed one dark alleyway we heard the unmistakable cry of a newborn baby. We looked at one another, not saying a word, and then found ourselves grinning from ear to ear. Breaking into a run – yes, even me with my dodgy hip – we headed for the half-open stable door.

Carol

O little town of Bethlehem

Reading

Luke 2:16-20

Reflection of the youngest shepherd

Looking back, I laugh at how awkward I felt, leaning over that manger, gazing at the red-faced little baby. I wasn't much more than a kid myself, not married, and with precious little experience of babies, seeing as how I was the youngest of four. And now, decades after the event, what I remember most isn't the smell of baby sick mixed with cow dung; it isn't the expression on the face of the baby's mother when Zebulun told her that we'd been sent by an angel; it's the memory of my doubts at the sight of that baby, so tiny, so helpless, almost swamped by the swaddling bands and the heaps of fresh straw on which he lay. Was this really the Saviour, Christ the Lord, the promised one? The one who would grow up to save us from the Romans, to bring a better way of life, to make sure that people like us got a bit of respect and a better deal? If he was, then we were going to have a long wait. And probably by the time he was grown up, he'd be doing all the things lordly people do – living in a palace, issuing orders and edicts and ignoring the poor.

And yet angels don't get things wrong – not that I had spoken to any before that night, but I knew that they came from God and God knows everything. So perhaps, if this really was the Christ, the Messiah, born to ordinary people who, judging by their clothes weren't exactly rolling in money – well then, maybe he really would get it. Maybe he would grow up to understand what the daily grind was really like, to realise that just because a person hasn't got a lot, doesn't mean their thoughts and longings aren't just as important as the guy who parades about in fine robes and eats off golden platters. And if he got that, then who was to say he couldn't change things? Sort out the Romans, make the bosses give us a living wage, even make the law a bit more fair so that it wasn't always the people who couldn't afford lawyers who got the raw end of the deal.

118

It was when Zebulun dug me in the ribs that I realised I was day-dreaming again. I did a lot of that back then – well, to be honest I've always been a bit of dreamer, making up stories in my head, wondering how things would pan out if I could call the shots. But even I, in my wildest imaginings, didn't for one second realise the impact that tiny newborn Jesus was going to have on my life.

And if I had, I wonder whether I wouldn't have been scared half to death.

Silence

Carol

See him lying on a bed of straw (*Oh, now carry me to Bethlehem*)

Reflection of the shepherd's wife

You can't blame me for not believing my husband at first. It seemed such a far-fetched yarn – an angel holding a conversation with a group of ragamuffin shepherds! What did he take me for? To be honest, I was pretty sharp with him – worry does that to me, and I'd had enough to fret about that week. I hadn't got round to telling Zeb yet but I'd lost my job a couple of days earlier: well, I call it a job, but they only used me down at the inn when no one else was available – they said I was getting too slow and clumsy. I guess I proved them right: the place was packed, what with the census and everything, so they grudgingly let me work. And what did I do? Dropped a pile of crocks on the stone floor and then stumbled and sent a dish of stuffed vine leaves flying across the room. That was it. No more work for me.

I'd hardly slept a wink, worrying about how we were going to manage, so Zeb crashing in at first light with his tales of heavenly visions was the last straw. And when he started on about being sent to find some special baby – well, I told him to come down to earth and live in the real world and then I stormed out. I suppose I was just avoiding telling him the bad news.

But then I thought I'd give it one more try. Go to the inn, grovel, apologise, offer to do anything at all for even less pay than I had been getting. One lepton was better than nothing.

I was making my way to the back entrance – no point irritating the boss by using the guest entrance – when I saw the outhouse. Well, I mean, I've seen it a dozen times before – I've worked 50 yards from it for heaven's sake. But there was a light flickering and I could see the outline of a man walking up and down past the door. And that was unusual. Maybe if I could tell the boss that some no good tramp was using his outhouse, he'd be grateful and give me my job back.

That was when I heard the high-pitched yell of a very furious baby.

A baby in a feeding trough. Zeb's words echoed in my head and I edged closer till I could hear the man's voice trying desperately to soothe the baby. And making a pig's ear of it.

I stuck my head round the door. A young woman, pale from lack of sleep, was wringing her hands and looked close to tears.

'What shall we do, Joseph? He's been fed, he's warm, he's . . .'

'Give him your finger to suck.' The words were out of my mouth before I knew it. The two of them looked up in shock.

'Sorry,' I blurted out. 'But that stops them yelling. They just need to suck for comfort, you see, even when they're not hungry.'

The woman took the baby and put her little finger in his mouth. He hiccupped a couple of times and then began noisily sucking, his tiny eyelids drooping as a huge sigh of relief escaped from his little chest.

'Thank you!' The woman looked up at me and smiled. I nodded and turned to go; baby or no baby, they were trespassing and I wanted my job back.

I was halfway across the yard when I realised I couldn't do it. It wasn't just that I kept thinking back to my own little ones – the three I'd lost and the four who were now caring for kids of their own – it was what Zeb had tried to tell me about angels and the baby they'd found being someone really special – a Saviour for us all, Zeb said.

Suddenly, the job didn't matter. I picked up my skirt and ran back down the street to my house. I wanted him to tell me again, from the very beginning, and this time I wouldn't make fun of him. I would just listen.

Silence

Hymn

While shepherds kept their watching (*Go tell it on the mountain*)

Reflection of a night shelter user at the back of the church

I've only come here because the night shelter doesn't open for another hour. It's warm here and no one seems to mind. They've got one of those Nativity scenes here, just like the one set up near the serving hatch at the night shelter. Theirs is a bit more chipped than this one: Joseph's nose has been knocked off and the donkey's got an ear missing, but it's kind of nice. It reminds me of – oh, it reminds me of so much.

It reminds me of when I was a small kid and Christmas meant a tree and presents and singing carols round the estate and spending the money on sweets. And then getting ticked off for not giving it to charity. (Ironic that – now I am the charity.)

It reminds me of school Nativity plays when I was one of those shepherds – wearing my tatty dressing gown and one of my nan's tea towels on my head and wishing I could be like Nathan White and be one of the Wise Men with a velvet jacket and a crown and carry a big box of gold which didn't really have gold in it but chocolate biscuits which you got to share on the last day of term.

It reminds me of the year when it all started to go wrong. That was just before Christmas time too – and I so wanted to be one of the gang. My mum's latest boyfriend hated my guts and didn't mind using his fists to prove it and I had started at secondary school – in the remedial class, of course. Thicko they called me and that was when they were feeling polite. So when a couple of the cool guys started being friendly and saying I could join their gang if I could prove myself – well, I didn't need to sit and think about it. I wanted in.

It was downhill from there. All they wanted me for was as their fall guy, the one who fetched the drugs, the one who acted as decoy while they thieved, the one who in the end the police caught with the blood-stained knife hidden in his pants.

They had a crib like this down the young offenders' place. There was a chaplain there who held classes; I didn't go. I reckoned a God who could let a 16-year-old take the blame for something he didn't do and not step in to sort things out wasn't worth wasting time on.

When I got out, I fell in with this girl, Mandy. We didn't get married but we had a couple of kids. Only by then the drugs were calling me again, and she had a couple of suppliers and got me hooked on the harder stuff and they took the kids off us. She died. An injection that went wrong. I ended up on the streets.

You know the weirdest thing? I thought that was it – life over, trashed. Thought I was a total loser, and I might as well end it all. Then a guy at this place told me that you could get free food and drink every Sunday at some community centre the other side of town. Run by churches, he said. Well, that put me off, I can tell you, but I went because he said the ham sandwiches were great and you got a bowl of soup as well, all for nothing.

Oh yeah, I know what you're thinking. Happy-ever-after ending. He found God and now he's as pure as the driven snow. I haven't found God. But you know what? I've found people who have. People who look me in the eye and shake my hand and ask me how things are going and sound like they really care. I've been going for a few weeks now. This week they're having a bit of a Christmas service. They want me to go.

I don't know. I mean, I'm not really the sort. Not with my record – not with all the things I've said to and about God.

I'm not the holy sort.

But then again, those shepherds – they were pretty down and out if I remember the story rightly. I wonder if seeing the baby Jesus made any difference to their lives. I guess not. I guess they had to go right back to those sheep and carry on day after day in the same dreary routine. Still, they had one over the rest of their mates, didn't they? They got written about in the Bible, and that's something you can't say for many people.

I might go. Just hover on the edge, you know, just to sing the carols – I like singing and I've not got a bad voice even though I say so myself. There's a guy there who reckons he's going to get a group together to sing down the shopping mall on Christmas Eve.

I might give it a go. Nothing to lose. Because when all's said and done, it's not a bad story, is it? Angels talking to poor men and telling them the secret before any of the toffee-nosed lot have a clue what's going on.

I might go. Just for the singing. No harm in that, is there? You never know, it might be kind of nice.

And they say there'll be mince pies after.

Prayers of intercession

Lord Jesus, your first visitors were so right, so appropriate because they heralded the way you would live your earthly life. You mixed with those whom your society regarded as the dregs, and you loved them. Not just a pat on the head, penny in the collecting tin, kind of love but true love. Love that gave and gave, love that didn't do a risk assessment before venturing into the seamy areas of town, love that talked for as long as someone needed to hear a kindly voice. But your love was also a tough love – a love that required people to change, to mend their ways, to follow a different path. As we face the challenges of our broken world today, may we understand that it is not just those on the street corners, those in the police cells and those whose bodies are being destroyed by drugs, drink or self-abuse who need to change: *it is us too*. We need to look at the world and at our brothers and sisters through your eyes, and it's hard, Lord. Really, really hard. And so we pray that you would help us to eliminate our prejudice, get over our super-sensitivity and reach out in love to those for whom the word has little meaning. It's too big a challenge, Lord, for us to cope with unless you walk alongside us. But you do and we will, with your help, continue to try. Amen.

(*Here follow intercessory prayers for the congregation, community and wider world.*)

Hymn

Jesus Christ is waiting

Blessing and dismissal

12

Send in the angels

A service for the Sunday following Christmas Day

This is recommended for use when Christmas Day falls between Monday and Thursday. It is recommended that the words of Mary should be read by a young woman and those of the struggling worshipper by an older woman.

Introduction

How honest are we about our worship lives? Do we speak in glowing terms of the uplifting joy, the indescribable peace, the deep conviction that our faith gives us – and keep quiet about the rest of it? About the times in the bleak pit of despair, when God seems so far away that maybe we only imagined him in the first place? The times when all the praying seems futile because not only does nothing change, but our hearts get heavier and our doubts look larger? Do we keep quiet about all those times because we want to be seen as 'good Christians', and apparently 'good Christians' are upbeat 24/7?

Do we imagine that the people who figure so prominently in the Christmas story were somehow relieved of all feelings of fear, doubt, panic, emptiness and pain? Do we really, truly believe that the God who valued humanity so much that he sent his one and only Son to live as a human among humans, somehow magically removed all human emotion from his chosen family?

Our God waits, as he always has and always will, to receive our prayers, our panics, our anger and our despair and to transform them with gentleness and love. But he will not do that until we bring them all, willingly, freely to him.

Reading

Luke 2:1-8, 15-20

Reflection of Mary

He was so beautiful, my son Jesus. The moment I held him, I loved him with a love I wouldn't have felt possible. I just wanted to stare and stare at him, this precious gift from God. When those shepherds came, Joseph was all for sending them packing but I just wanted to show Jesus off – and, of course, when they told us about the angels – well – that just heightened the whole sense of wonder, the awesome miracle we were part of. I felt invincible.

The feeling didn't last.

He cried. Oh, how he cried. Whenever I managed to nod off, he would begin that high-pitched piercing howl. He seemed to need feeding every five minutes and then he would dirty himself and need cleaning and by the time I'd done that and fallen asleep, the whole thing would start over. It wasn't so bad for Joseph; he seemed able to sleep through the yelling and, in the daytime, he would go to the house of his cousin Benjamin and collect food for us; of course, I couldn't go for seven days because I was unclean. I knew he needed space – time to get used to this massive change in our lives – but to be honest, I got a bit low by the fourth day; I kept bursting into tears and wondering whether I could cope with this awesome, mind-blowing responsibility. I tried telling myself that God had entrusted his Son to me and so he would tell me what to do but repeating that over and over didn't stop the baby crying – or me, for that matter.

I'm ashamed to say that one morning, after Joseph had gone out, and Jesus was demanding more food and my nipples were throbbing and my head aching, I cried out to God, 'I can't do this – I don't know how to care for him.' I guess I must have really shouted because an elderly woman put her head round the door and smiled and asked if she could help. Meeting her was a turning point; she was such a help, telling me not to worry about Jesus' crying and showing me how to soothe him and bring up his wind. I'm glad I had her; to be honest, I wonder how I would have coped during that time without her; I felt so homesick and just wanted my family around me. I guess that's why God sent Shamira – to tell me all the practical stuff that angels don't mention.

Because of her, I began to feel better. For a while.

Carol

Infant holy, infant lowly *or* See him lying on a bed of straw

Reading

Psalm 31:1-5, 9, 10, 14-16

Reflection of a weary worshipper

(The references to various services and activities may be adapted to suit the situation.)

Well, here I am again, Lord. It seems like I've been back and forth to church for days on end – what with all the Advent services, and the crib service with the grandchildren, and the carol service, and the Midnight . . . and it was all lovely and the choir were really great and the church looked wonderful and yet . . . and yet I feel so guilty, Lord. I feel all Christmas-ed out.

In fact, I'm not at all sure that I like Christmas all that much.

Oh, don't get me wrong, Lord. I loved having my family with me, honestly I did. Family are a gift from you, and I am truly grateful that they want to be with me – there are so many people of my age who sit alone on Christmas Day and who would give anything to see even one friendly face. And I did do all the things that mums and grannies do at Christmas – everyone liked their presents, which was a relief considering how much they cost; the turkey was cooked to perfection; and we didn't run out of wine. The meals were all on time, I played on the Wii Fit with my grandson till my knees ached, and lost just the right number of times at Snakes and Ladders with the little ones. I didn't flinch (well not much) when they tramped mud up the stairs or left all the lights on or spilt squash on the duvet. I even held my tongue when they pointed out that I was repeating myself, or that it was time I slowed down and stopped rushing around like a headless chicken.

It was lovely to have them.

And the worship at church was as wonderful as ever – the familiar story, the carols, the children in their tea towels and dressing gowns for the Nativity play, the candles burning for Midnight Communion. And me doing all the things that were expected of a good church-warden: attending every service, welcoming newcomers, stepping in to do whatever was needed. I smiled so much that my face ached. I smiled so they wouldn't see the big black hole inside.

The hole wasn't about the worship or the family.

The hole was – is – about me. Or, more precisely, you and me. That's why I feel guilty, Lord. Guilty because it's been Christmas – and you know what? I spent less time talking to you, less time on my knees, less time even trying to think holy thoughts than at any other time of the year. My prayers amounted to a quick 'Give me strength, Lord' or the odd 'Please don't let me forget to defrost the mince pies'; my reading of Scripture was hardly more than a rapid scan of the verses on the Christmas cards or a flick through The Story of Christmas for the Under Fives; and as for thanksgiving, it was more a quick word of gratitude for an unburnt turkey or a sleeping toddler than any reference to your most precious gift of the infant Christ.

And then there were my innermost thoughts, Lord. The moments I yearned to be part of a couple again, to have someone beside me to share, not just the hard work, but the joy and the fun; someone to curl up with at night and reflect on the day. I looked at my children with their husbands and partners and for a moment, I was envious, Lord. I'm ashamed to admit it but it's true.

On the other hand, there were the times when I yearned for just 10 minutes of utter quiet and stillness; the times when, unbidden, that dread sentence that I vowed I would never think came into my head: 'If he was my child, he wouldn't get away with that.' Which of course is a lot of nonsense because when I was a mother with three children under five, my lot got away with far worse. And then, Lord, when they did all go out for a walk and I had half an hour to myself, what did I do? Read the Bible? Meditate on your word? Pray? No. I ate chocolate and worried about how much I had spent and watched EastEnders on iPlayer.

And now here I am again, Lord. Back in church. On my knees – and that's an effort that it never used to be. And try as I might, I can't find you. That feeling of stillness, of closeness to your presence that I used to get isn't there. The tree with its twinkling lights, the decorations made by the Sunday school, the crib with its straw and tiny lifelike baby serve only to irritate me – I want them to be packed away so that they can no longer make me feel at such odds with my surroundings. And even as I think that, I find myself pleading under my breath, begging you to help me, to lift this blackness and give me back the joy that when I did have it, I took for granted.

And still you are silent.

Oh, I don't blame you – after all, for days I haven't given you the full-on attention you deserve; even when I was singing carols, I was mentally counting Brussels sprouts or worrying about the daughter who seemed out of sorts with me. So I don't blame you that you've gone quiet on me. Only I need you, Lord; I need you so much. Because this is crunch time, Father. The black pit of depression is drawing ever closer. And it scares me so much.

See, I can't go on doing what I've been doing for so long, God. I can't keep up this image of the totally sure, totally together Christian who leads intercessions, runs house groups, reads the lesson – all the time giving the impression of someone who has got it sussed.

Because, I haven't, Lord. I don't get why when I need you most you are silent; when I scream at you at the top of my voice, all I hear echoing back at me is silence. You called me, I'm sure of that. You're the one who got me to this place and I'm grateful for it. But now I'm calling *you*, Lord; begging you to show me a way ahead, a way out of the deep, muddy pit that I feel is threatening to swallow me up. Begging you to give me back the energy I once had, to restore the enthusiasm and the vigour and – well, yes, Lord – to give me back the certainty that I am worth something still and that you still have a plan and a purpose for me to fulfil, flawed, and wavering and inadequate as I am.

You sent an angel to Mary; you sent one to Joseph. You sent one to Zechariah, even though he messed up by doubting and questioning.

Couldn't you possibly, Lord, send one to me? Before it's too late.

Silence

Prayer

(The response from the congregation is in bold type.)

Lord, we give you our pain. **Take it, transform it, we pray.**
Lord, we give you our anger. **Take it, transform it, we pray.**
Lord, we give you our disappointment. **Take it, transform it, we pray.**
Lord, we give you our loneliness. **Take it, transform it, we pray.**
Lord, we give you ourselves. **Take us, transform us, show us the way.**
This we so earnestly pray. Amen.

Reading

Psalm 31:1-5, 9, 10, 14-16

Hymn

Courage, brother, do not stumble *or* Longing for light, we wait in darkness (*Christ be our light*)

Reading

Luke 2:22-38

Reflection of Mary

I had expected it to be a day of the greatest joy and rejoicing. I had thought that I would be over the moon, on cloud nine; to be at the Temple for my purification, to present our son to the priest – and then return home, and show off my beautiful baby. I knew Joseph was still struggling to get his head around all that had happened, worrying that all he could afford to offer at the Temple was a couple of small pigeons – a lamb was out of the question on our budget. Even doves were too pricey. And that wasn't the only thing that was stressing him out; all the way to the Temple, he kept saying that he loved Jesus but he didn't feel that he was his real father; that God had chosen me but he, Joseph the neighbourhood carpenter, felt like an outsider in all this amazing business. I didn't know what to say – the anxiety in his face tugged at my heartstrings. Before I knew it, I heard myself scolding him in the way my mother used to scold me.

'Now listen,' I said, 'enough of all that. God chose me – but he chose you too. He chose you to be Jesus' earthly father – day in, day out, through good times and bad, for as long as it takes. He chose you to be the one to teach him the Torah, play games with him, teach him your craft. Doesn't that tell you that God has faith in you, that he'll be right with you every step of the way? So stop worrying.'

He stopped dead in his tracks and looked straight into my eyes. And in that moment I think we both knew that those words came from my lips but they had been put there by God himself. I felt a wave of joy wash over me and saw every muscle in Joseph's dear face relax into a broad smile. By the time we reached the Gate of Nicanor at the entrance to the Temple, Joseph seemed more at peace than he had done for weeks.

And that is why I hesitated when he asked me what was troubling me as we left the Temple hours later after the consecration. I said I was tired, that it had been a big day, that I was short on sleep. But Joseph wasn't fooled. He pressed me for an answer – so I said Simeon had said that Jesus had been chosen by God and that he would save many souls. And it was true; that was part of what he had said and I hoped it would be enough to satisfy Joseph. It wasn't.

'That's a good and wonderful thing,' he said. 'So what else? What else is troubling you?'

How could I tell him? How could I tell him that Simeon had said people would speak out against Jesus? That he had taken my hand and whispered – *'and a sword will pierce your own soul too.'* When the priest had spoken those words I had felt for a moment as though every vein in my body was being flooded with ice cold water. I couldn't burden Joseph with that. Not after everything he had done for me.

So I pretended it was the old lady who had got to me. The one who had kept watching us and pointing us out to everyone. I told Joseph I had felt embarrassed and wondered what she was saying about us. He laughed and said there was nothing to worry about; that one of the priests had told him her name was Anna and she lived in the Temple.

'She kept telling everyone that Jesus was a gift from God, and would be the Saviour of us all,' Joseph told me. 'Nothing nasty, nothing to worry about.'

And I smiled and nodded and never told him about the sword that was going to pierce my very soul one day.

Never.

Hymn

When Mary brought her treasure *or* Of the Father's love begotten

Reflection of a weary worshipper

How did she do that, Lord? How did Mary carry those words of Simeon inside her head and her heart all those years? How did she feel when Jesus began his ministry, because she must have heard all the backbiting and sniping, must have known that the authorities were out to get him, and those words would have come back to haunt her.

But she had no choice, did she, Lord? From the moment she said 'Let it be' she knew it was out of her hands. She could only love and watch and wait and pray. Did she weep in private when Jesus was hounded out of the synagogue in his own town? Did she do what I do – shout at you and ask what you were thinking of? And when he was betrayed, arrested, tortured, flogged and then nailed to a cross of wood – what were her prayers of anguish and agony then? Did she still trust you one hundred per cent, every minute of every hour? Was there never one moment of unrestrained fury at what you were allowing to happen?

I am sure there was. But somehow her faith, her love for you, her love for her son – your Son – was greater than the anger, stronger than the fear, more ingrained than the desire to retaliate and fight back.

I think I am beginning to get it, Lord. When we turn to you and open our hearts and lives to you, we open ourselves to all that you have planned – and we don't get a set of instructions telling us what to expect next. Not every moment can be one of peace and joy, even if the calendar says it should be. Not every angel that you send appears in a blaze of dazzling light wearing robes as white as a detergent advert. Maybe the anger and resentment I'm feeling about your apparent absence has, in reality, nothing to do with you at all. Perhaps it is me I'm angry with – and perhaps by holding the space, and being quiet, you are gently, lovingly, leading me to the point when I can acknowledge that.

Because, yes, Lord, I'm angry. Angry that at times my children lead their lives in ways that seem to me totally crazy; angry that the days are long gone when they need me to sort out their problems. And, yes, angry that I can't do as much as I once did; that I do from time to time repeat myself, forget what someone has told me, wish that the pace of life would slow down a bit. Angry that sometimes I get my priorities all skewed and worry more about what people will think than what you will think, more about making a good impression than stopping long enough to hear your still, small voice of calm. Angry, in short, that I am not in charge.

Forgive me, Father. Forgive my pride that puts looking efficient and successful before sitting with you. Forgive my impatience that makes me want instant answers and a perpetually happy frame of mind. Help me to see that these black moments actually do draw me closer to you because in my fear and my fury I open up to you – albeit by shouting and crying! And when I do, you respond – as you have now, by word and story, by a phrase in a hymn or simply by sending a thought unbidden into my mind and allowing the turmoil to cease just for a moment or two.

I don't know when the depression will lift, Lord. But you do. I haven't a clue what you want of me next, Lord. But you do. I don't know how I am going to learn that I need to change the way I do things. But you do.

Perhaps all I need to do right now is absolutely nothing. Nothing other than to say from the bottom of my heart, 'O holy child of Bethlehem, descend to me, I pray. Cast out my sin, and enter in; be born in me today.'

Carol

O little town of Bethlehem

Prayers

Father God, as we continue to rejoice in the birth of your newborn son, we, like all families with new children, need to take time to settle into a new way of life. Just as for Mary and Joseph, Christmas was only the beginning of their life with your Son, so may we move on from the easy images of baby Jesus into the challenge that living with him brings into our lives. Give us strength when following him leads us into unfamiliar territory; be with us in our moments of fear, steady us when turning away from you seems an easier option than following you and hold us, Father, when we cannot see a way to be.

Lord, in your mercy, hear our prayer.

Father, this period between Christmas Day and the resumption of normal life can often feel rather like limbo. We seem to be waiting. We pray that as the Wise Men waited to arrive at Bethlehem, and as Mary and Joseph waited to discover the next part of their story, so we may take the time to wait for what will unfold for us in this New Year.

At this time of year many of us make the same resolutions as we failed to keep last year. God of hope and strength, we pray that whatever else we may have in mind to do in this new year, we may earnestly seek to follow you more closely, and listen for your word guiding us.

Lord, in your mercy, hear our prayer.

We pray for a more peaceful time in those areas of our world racked by instability, whether caused by war, terrorism, natural disasters or changes in government.

Particularly at this moment we pray for . . .

Lord, you who were prophesied to be the Prince of Peace, guide those in positions of earthly power towards more peaceful resolutions of these crises.

Lord, in your mercy, hear our prayer.

So as we stand, still within the Christmas season, but moving on into the New Year, may we, with Mary, Joseph, the shepherds and the Wise Men, welcome you into this world, and into our lives, and resolve to walk with you into whatever the coming year may offer us.

Merciful Father, accept these prayers for the sake of your Son, our Saviour Jesus Christ. Amen.

Hymn

Lord for the years

Blessing and dismissal

May the God of grace grant to us peace in perplexity, calm in times of trouble, hope in his promises and joy in the knowledge of his unfailing understanding of our needs at all times. And now may the blessing of God Almighty, the Father, Son and Holy Spirit, be upon us all and remain with us and those whom we love, this day and for evermore. **Amen.**

13

Come, Lord Jesus

A service of readings, reflections and carols

Call to worship

We have come. Come just as we are – some of us eager, excited, filled with the joy of the season, some of us anxious, fearful, trying so hard to suppress the pain of an empty Christmas, a Christmas without those we love, a Christmas filled with pain of sickness or past hurts.

We have come searching. Some of us searching for that dimly remembered thrill at the sound of the first carol; some of us searching for a friendly face who will see and understand our pain and acknowledge it with a smile and not with elaborate words of pity.

We have come, each of us unique in our longing – some of us happy to brave the darkness of a December night, some of us carrying within our own darkness, the darkness of fear, of wondering whether we still believe, the darkness of wondering whether you still care.

We have come.

And will you come here tonight, Lord? We see the inert, unmoving form of your infant self, a well-made doll in a crib crafted by the churchwarden, and we know the story so well. But it's not enough, Lord. Will you come here tonight and embrace us all – the happy and the grieving, those who search and feel inadequate, those who have found and still wonder whether there is more? Will you come tonight, Lord, and enter our hearts, still our fears, fill our emptiness, ease our guilt?

We ask in hope, in trust, with pleading and with expectation.

For you are God and you will come.

Reading

(*To be repeated four times from four different areas of the worship space. The four voices should, if possible, include a young child, a young adult, a more mature adult and a very elderly adult – both male and female.*)

'For God so loved the world that he gave his one and only Son, that whoever believes in him shall not perish but have eternal life.'

Short silence

Hymn

O come, O come, Emmanuel

Reading

Matthew 1:18-23

Reflection of Joseph

(The words of the angel in this reflection may be spoken out of sight of the congregation if required.)

I don't know which was stronger – my anger or my grief. That Mary, my own beloved, precious Mary, should be with child – a child that wasn't mine! All my dreams for the future smashed into a thousand pieces – how could she? How could she do it to me?

I remember running and running, away from the village and up into the hills, stumbling on the rocky path, until the stitch in my side vied with the pain in my heart. Finally I could run no more, and I veered off the path into an olive grove and sank to the ground, beating my fists against my head and yes – I confess – crying like a kid. I wanted to be sick; I wanted to hit someone; I wanted to grab hold of Mary and shake her and make her tell me what she had been thinking of.

But despite all that anger and grief, something inside told me that Mary couldn't have, wouldn't have, betrayed me. A thousand images began tumbling through my head. Did she meet some opportunist lout while she was away? But surely Elizabeth and Zechariah would have kept her close to them and besides, no Jewish boy known to such a priestly family would dare . . . oh dear God! The Romans! Had one of them done this to her? Had she been raped?

However it had happened, one thing was clear. I had to divorce her. No self-respecting Jew with a reputation and a business to protect could be seen to have any dealings with a woman who allowed herself to be used like that. But what if it wasn't her fault?

Suddenly I was overcome with a weariness beyond anything I had felt before. I closed my eyes and was drifting into a tortured sleep when I sensed someone dropping to the ground beside me and laying a hand on my shoulder. I tried to focus but the sinking sun was shining directly into my eyes. Try as I would, I couldn't open my eyes wide enough to see who was there.

Angel Joseph, Joseph, you're a descendant of David, right? So put all thoughts of denouncing and divorcing Mary out of your mind right now! The baby she is carrying isn't the result of anything bad or immoral that's happened to her.

Joseph I forced my eyes open, trying to frame words in my head but it seemed my lips wouldn't move. The man beside me seemed to be shimmering in a heat haze; in fact he didn't really resemble any of the men from around Nazareth.

Angel Mary has done nothing wrong. The child she is carrying has been conceived by God's Holy Spirit. It is God's Son she is carrying.

Joseph Again I opened my mouth but couldn't utter a single word.

Angel Mary will have a little boy and you have been chosen by God to be his earthly father. You will call him Jesus because he will be the one who saves people; saves them from all their wrongdoing and misguided ways and sinful behaviour.

Joseph By now the guy was leaning so close to me that I could feel his breath on my cheek, drying the moisture of my tears. I wanted to shout and tell him he was an idiot but then he said something that made my heart miss a beat.

Angel All this is happening so that what the prophets said might be brought to fruition: a virgin will be pregnant and bear a son and they shall call his name Emmanuel, which means God with us. You do remember?

Joseph Well, of course I did – what Jewish guy whose parents brought him up in the faith wouldn't remember the prophecy about the Messiah who would save them. But here? Now? And . . . me? Us?
The man touched my arm and my flesh tingled.

Angel God is with you, Joseph. He has chosen you, just as he has chosen Mary. So put away your fears, ignore the gossips and do as God wants. It's OK. Don't be afraid.

Joseph Don't be afraid? What was the man on? 'Hang on!' I shouted, relief pouring over me as I realised I could suddenly speak. I sat bolt upright and looked around. He had gone. And the ground where he had been sitting bore no imprint. The grass was as straight as it had always been.

Hymn

Father, I place into your hands *or* I do not know what lies ahead

Prayer

For the times when our dreams lie broken and discarded, we pray your comfort, Lord. For the times when our anger frightens us and threatens to overpower us, we pray your calming, Lord. For the times when in our bleakness we can see no way ahead, we pray your light, Lord. And in all our times of our aloneness, we pray for the realisation of your presence holding us, Lord. Amen.

Reading

Luke 1:26-38

Reflection (for female voices)

First voice I'd known her all my life. We'd grown up in the same street, Mary and I. We'd played together when we were small, grumbled about our chores as we got older and giggled together when we both became betrothed within a month of one another.

And then she changed. It came out of the blue. One day she was her normal self, and the next she was like a different person. Quiet – and Mary had never been quiet in her life! I would see her at the well and we'd start to chat and then suddenly she would get this faraway look in her eyes and I could tell she wasn't listening to a word I was saying.

Second voice *(Mary)* The thoughts kept falling over one another in my head. I was going to have a baby. I was going to have a baby and I wasn't married. I was going to have a baby who would be God's own Son. I couldn't understand how – or why it should be me. But I believed it. I believed it with my whole heart. And I also knew that no one else would believe for one second.

What would I say to my family? My friends? To Joseph? I needed someone to talk to and much as I loved her, I knew my friend Judith was not the right person. She would think I'd been out in the sun too long, and she'd begin teasing me about being a dreamer and I couldn't take that, not right then. And then I remembered.

Elizabeth. The angel had said Elizabeth was expecting a child too. That seemed even more incredible than my own pregnancy – my cousin was old, too old to conceive. But if anyone would understand my confusion and my anxieties, she would.

That's when I decided. I would go to her. Tell her everything. And she would tell me how to break the news to Joseph.

Carol

The Angel Gabriel from heaven came

Reading

Luke 1:39-45

Reflection of Elizabeth

I don't have the words to describe how it felt. Don't get me wrong, I had believed that I was pregnant ever since Zechariah came home from the Temple, struck dumb and wild-eyed, scribbling on his wax tablet the story of the angel and the mind-blowing news that I, whose monthly flow had all but ceased, was to be a mother at last. Oh yes, I had believed – the sickness each morning, the overpowering craving for figs in the middle of each night, the thickening around my waist – all sure signs.

But the day that my cousin Mary arrived from Nazareth – that was something else. I had hurried into the courtyard at the sound of the cart drawing up outside, and as Mary came through the archway, her face lighting up with that familiar smile that dimpled her cheeks the way it had since she was a tiny baby, I felt this great somersault deep inside me. My baby! For a few days I had felt tiny flutters, so insignificant as to make me wonder whether it was my imagination, but this was no flutter – this felt like a fish leaping out of the water and splashing back again, the way you see on the lake some days. I felt tears spring to my eyes – that this should be happening to me and at the same time as Mary . . .

In that moment, without anyone having spoken a word, I knew that Mary too was pregnant.

'Oh Mary, you are so so blessed,' I said, 'and the baby you're carrying – he is – what can I say? God's gift to us! And now you, the mother of my Lord, are here in my house? What have I done to deserve such joy?'

Mary looked at me in amazement, and asked me how on earth I knew she was with child, so I told her about how my baby had leapt for joy when she arrived. And then I said something else.

I said, 'Mary – you too have been chosen by God. I don't know how I know, I just do! I am right, aren't I?'

Mary nodded and impulsively I grasped her hands and twirled her round, laughing out loud with the sheer joy of it all.

'Isn't God the most amazing, most wonderful Father of us all?' I cried. 'Are we not truly blessed?'

Hymn

I cannot tell *or* O what a mystery I see

Reading

Luke 2:1-7

Reflection for two voices

First voice   They went because someone in power said they had to. It wasn't convenient; it wasn't part of their plan. After all, there was a business to run, orders to be met, money to be earned. But they went. They had no choice.

Second voice   They went because that was part of your plan. Not the emperor's – yours. Maybe they didn't realise that then; all they knew was that despite the inconvenience, and the worry and the discomfort, you had chosen them and promised to be with them. And that was enough.

First voice   Perhaps they thought that with you in charge, everything would be made easy; everything would work out just fine, everything would fall into place and that you would make the path ahead smooth and pothole free. Home in plenty of time for the birth, a quick labour, surrounded by loving family and friends. But it didn't work out like that.

Second voice   Was Mary alarmed and fearful when those first contractions hit her with the force of a boulder in the pit of her stomach?

First voice   Did Joseph panic as time began to run out and still there was no place to rest?

Second voice   How did they know what to do?

First voice   So far from home, with no experience of delivering a child and no family nearby to encourage and comfort.

Second voice   Did you send someone, God, to lend a hand? Someone the Gospel writers forgot to mention? Or did you just leave them to go it alone?

First voice   Or did Mary cry out in pain and did a neighbour hear her distress? Did anyone come, Lord, at your birth?

Reading

(Extract from *The Greatest Love Story Ever Told – And Then Some!* by Rosie Rushton, published by Kevin Mayhew)

Joseph ran ahead, shouting for help while Mary, panting for breath and reciting every prayer she had ever learned, leant against the donkey, which conveniently seemed more interested in a clump of grass than his mistress' distress.

'Help me, please! I can feel the baby, it's coming, I know it's coming.' Mary cried.

'Now don't you worry, my dear!' An elderly woman, as wide as she was high, bustled over to Mary, cast an experienced eye over her and turned to Joseph, who had turned back at the sound of her voice.

'What were you thinking of, dragging this poor lass about in her condition?' the woman demanded. 'Honestly, you men – you don't have a clue!'

'Aaarghhh!' Mary's cry of agony froze any reply that Joseph might have made. Wrapping his arm around her, he took all her weight and together they stumbled along, following the woman around the back of a small house.

'I'm Shamira,' the woman said. 'And you are lucky – I am a midwife!'

Relief flooded Mary's face.

'I can't have you inside my house,' Shamira went on apologetically. 'My husband's mother died last night and our spare room is full of relatives – besides, you will need food. But you can stay here.'

She gestured to a crumbling stone shelter built onto the side of the house.

'Matthias built that in the days when we had more animals than we could manage downstairs,' she sniffed. 'But these days, what with the taxes and the Romans . . .'

Her words were drowned out in another groan from Mary whose face was beaded with sweat.

'It's coming!'

'I will get water,' Shamira said hastily, turning to Joseph. 'And you – lay her down on the straw and I'll get her a blanket.'

'Thank you,' Mary gasped 'Thank you so much.'

'Don't you bother thanking me,' the woman smiled. 'Just you get on and deliver that baby. My, but it's in a hurry. I shouldn't wonder if it's a girl – they always come fastest.'

'Oh no, it's a boy,' Mary replied.

'Bless her,' said the midwife winking at Joseph. 'Hope over experience, that's what that is. I know these things. Let's hope she's not disappointed. I'll go and get the water.'

Carol

It came upon the midnight clear *or* Once in royal David's city

Reading

Luke 2:8-14

Reflection of the Angel of the Lord

'Do not be afraid.' How often over the centuries have I and those like me uttered those words to frightened mortals! For you cannot get a message over to anyone until they feel safe – and sometimes it takes a while to calm them down – and then you need to repeat yourself over and over to make sure they've understood. It was no different that night – the night when he came, when God our heavenly and most awesome creator took on human form. Not just any human form but that of a tiny, vulnerable and totally dependent baby, which to be honest seemed to us a strange way of going about things when you consider he could have chosen any way he wanted to present himself to humankind. But God has always acted contrary to expectations – even heavenly ones!

What was more extraordinary was that we were to bring this life-changing news to a group of shepherds on a windswept hillside. Of course, the problem with that was that we – well, I, because to start with we reckoned the appearance of all of us in one fell swoop would finish them off! – the problem was that I preferred dealing with humans on a one-to-one basis. Get them in a crowd and fear spreads like wildfire – and that's what I was afraid would happen that night.

So I made a plan. I had seen a young boy – quite a lot younger than the rest – gazing at the stars with a look of awe and fascination on his face, and at once I knew he was the one I should appear to first. And I have to say it was a good choice; sure he jumped out of his skin and grabbed the arm of the shepherd sitting next to him, but he didn't back off and he didn't for one moment take his eyes off me.

We had made a connection, and with humans, that's always the right way to start.

Carol

Angels from the realms of glory *or* While shepherds watched

Reading

Luke 2:15-20

Reflection (for two voices)

First voice   Imagine that. Shepherds, the lowest of the low, the bottom of the pile, getting to be the first ones to hear about the birth of the Saviour.

Second voice   Strange, isn't it? They would have been grubby, smelly even – dirt under their fingernails, maybe even lice in their hair – and yet they got to be chosen to see Jesus, the newborn Saviour of the world, before anyone else at all.

First voice   No time to go and wash, put on clean clothes, make themselves presentable, the way we do before going to church. They just went as they were without a second thought because the angel told them to.

Second voice   But what about the ones they left behind? The shepherds who had to stay to watch the sheep and protect them from wolves? What did they feel like when their friends rushed off to witness this life-changing event – probably the biggest happening in Bethlehem since forever? How did they choose who would go to see Jesus and who would miss out?

First voice   Maybe they drew lots; maybe it was the youngest who got told to stay put. Someone had to stay behind. It stands to reason. But they'd have heard all about it when their mates returned.

Second voice And maybe they went themselves after that; maybe they visited the manger in relays and the Gospel writers didn't tell us because they thought it would be boring to keep repeating the same thing.

First voice   If the shepherds who went came back and told it like it really was, then the others would have just had to go. It stands to reason.

Second voice Some things are just too precious to ignore.

Carol

See him lying on a bed of straw *or* Away in a manger

Reading

Matthew 2:1-8

Reflection of one of the Wise Men

I didn't like him. They say you shouldn't make hasty judgements, but there was something about King Herod that made me very wary. Oh, at first he'd been affable enough, although I could tell by the way he eyed us up and down that he was working out whether we could be of any use to him. When we spoke of the star and explained that we were searching for the newborn King of the Jews, his whole demeanour changed; he sneered at us – we, who have spent our lives not just studying the stars but analysing ancient manuscripts and conversing with learned men of many faiths. But as we continued to speak, his eyes narrowed and I couldn't work out whether he was angry or frightened. Or both. Certainly, after he had called all his inner circle of cronies and counsellors to him and asked them what they made of our story, he was not a happy man. Oh, he smiled, and inclined his head graciously towards us when he spoke, but I could see that was all part of his manipulative game. He suddenly seemed keen to know every detail of the appearance of this new star; he told us his advisers had told him that it was predicted that a new ruler for Israel would be born in Bethlehem, a town just five miles away from Herod's palace in Jerusalem. 'Go there,' he said, 'and please, do come back and tell me exactly where he is, because then I must go at once and worship him too.'

At those words, the blood in my veins turned to ice, and even before the voice in my head shouted 'No!' I knew that we would never, under any circumstances, return to Jerusalem again.

Carol

We three kings of Orient are *or* As with gladness men of old *or* Three kings from Persian lands afar

Reflection of Mary

I was so confused. I couldn't get my head around everything that was happening. Only a few hours before, just as we were preparing to lie down for the night, three foreigners had turned up at the house bringing gifts beyond our wildest imaginings, telling us – well, telling Joseph, because actually I couldn't understand a word of their heavily accented attempts at Hebrew – telling him that they had followed a star and it had led them to us, to Jesus, whom they called the new King. We went outside the house, and there was the star: we hadn't noticed it before – but then, as Joseph said, maybe we didn't need to notice it. We already had Jesus with us. After they had left, we lay down to sleep – but within minutes Joseph was sitting bolt upright, shouting, sweat pouring off his brow.

'We must go,' he said. 'Now!' I told him it was a bad dream, begged him to go back to sleep – and then he told me. It was a dream, but he knew it was a dream from God. Herod wanted to kill our son. And what Herod wanted we all knew Herod got.

And so there we were, a few hours later, heading for the Egyptian border because that is where the Angel of the Lord had told us to go. What he hadn't told us was what to do when we got there, how long we had to be away from home, what on earth would happen to our house and business back in Nazareth.

About all that he hadn't said a word. So all we could do was trust and pray.

Silence

Prayers of intercession

Gracious Lord, let us never forget that embedded in the story of your coming in human form to our world, there are so many journeys. Journeys filled with excitement; journeys dogged by uncertainty; long journeys during which the outcome is uncertain; shorter journeys with unexpected diversions and problems. As we journey through our lives, Lord, may we never lose sight of you as our guide; when the signposts are muddied, speak to our hearts; when the road has more potholes than pavements, keep us from stumbling; and when we forget that through it all you are our ultimate and glorious destination, forgive us and lead us back into the right and only Way. Amen.

O Lord, who sent Jesus to be born in a stable in Bethlehem, we praise you for coming into this world as a child. As we ponder on the mystery of the God who became flesh and dwelt among us, open our hearts to receive you, open our lips to praise you and open our eyes to see your presence in the world today. Amen.

(*Here follow intercessory prayers for the congregation, community and wider world.*)

Carol

O come, all ye faithful *or* Hark, the herald-angels sing

Blessing and dismissal

14

Magi and massacre

A service for Epiphany

Introduction

During the season of Epiphany we think a great deal about the Magi who travelled hundreds of miles in their search for the newborn King of the Jews. Children dress up in robes, wear gold paper crowns on their heads and carry their treasures to lay at the foot of the crib before walking back through church or their school hall 'by another route' to signify that they are not returning to the court of King Herod.

Ah. Herod. He doesn't feature much in Nativity plays and certainly the actions he authorised – known now as the slaughter of the innocents – would not be seen as suitable material for young children. Yet it is an integral part of the Christmas story; one we ignore because it doesn't sit very comfortably with the image we have of the birth of Jesus. It is uncomfortable; it's disturbing and yes, it's not the sort of thing to re-enact in a Key Stage 1 school Nativity.

But we should not airbrush Herod out of the Christmas narrative because by reflecting on his reaction to the birth of Christ, we can face full-on the evil that still hovers over the world today. In Herod, we see the one who sells Thai children as prostitutes, or sends death squads out in the dead of night to slaughter those who don't agree with their regime. To ignore Herod is to dismiss the genocide and tyranny and violent abuse that, now as then, is a blot on the face of the world and the people that Christ came to save.

Carol

We three kings of Orient are

Reading

Matthew 2:1-6

Reflection of Herod's doorkeeper

Surely they'll be back soon. I mean, how long does it take to get to Bethlehem, have a bit of a recce and come back again? All this hanging about isn't doing me any good at all; every hour I get a message from King Herod demanding to know where they are – as if I have a clue!

Of course, he's only impatient because he's excited; so keen to go and meet this new king. And to think that I heard about him even before the high-ups at court! Of course, I'm Herod's right-hand man – well, that's how I like to think of myself despite what all the toffee-nosed, self-important advisers might tell you; they may have the learning and sneer at me because I'm just a slave – but it's me who can floor an ill-intentioned intruder in one fell swoop, me who opens the door to visitors and keeps them talking while they wait for an audience, me who frisks them to make sure there are no hidden knives or other unsavoury items concealed in their clothing.

Oh yes, I'm his right-hand man all right and I've met some strange people in my time here, but never have I come across a bunch quite like the foreigners who pitched up here a couple of weeks back. When I opened the door, you could have knocked me down with a feather – and for a moment I thought I'd lost the plot. I usually have a list of all the important people booked in to see the king and there was no note about these men. But it was obvious that they were no run of the mill opportunists. Their clothes, although dusty and travel-soiled, were opulent; their camels were well fed and their bearing – well, they looked like men who knew what they wanted and where they were going.

But they were clearly not Jews, and they definitely didn't come from these parts. That was obvious the moment their leader opened his mouth. Oh, he spoke Hebrew of sorts, but his accent was so thick that I struggled to understand him. Luckily, he had hired an interpreter and, between them, they got their message across and managed to tell me exactly who they were and what it was they wanted. Apparently they were astronomers and they'd found a star that signalled the birth of a new king, so they had upped sticks and set out to find him. It all seemed a bit foolhardy to me, especially when I heard that they had been on the journey for several months. Anyway, they thought that they'd find the baby here in Jerusalem, at the court, which seemed reasonable enough – but I knew there were no new babies in the palace, not unless you counted the cook's new son, but no way was he a king!

Of course, I went straight to Herod. Well, no, not to him exactly, but to his secretary, who went to his chief adviser, who went to Herod. Usually the king keeps visitors waiting for ages – he likes them nervous and deferential by the time they get to see him – but this time it was different. The summons came almost at once.

Reading

Matthew 2:7, 8

Reflection of one of the chief priests

Now let me be quite honest here; when Herod summoned me and a couple of my fellow priests into his inner chamber, I was pretty irritated. I had been deep in prayer – reflecting on the prophets and preparing for worship in the Temple the following day – and if there's one think I hate, it's to be disturbed from my time of silence.

But one doesn't disobey the king.

The moment we entered the room, I could see that Herod was agitated. He beckoned us over and gestured to a group of opulently dressed men seated across the room.

'This prophecy,' he said without so much as a greeting, 'the one about the coming of the Christ. Where is he to be born?'

My two colleagues glanced at me. This was a tricky question: not that we didn't know the answer – we were soaked in Scripture – but because Herod, for all his title of King of the Jews, wasn't Jewish; he was Idumaean and a puppet of the Romans. We all yearned for the time when the promised Messiah would come and champion our cause, deliver us from oppression and bring in a new age of peace. We also knew that Herod wouldn't share that vision one little bit.

'Well, tell me!' he shouted.

'Sire, the prophet Micah tells us quite clearly that he will be born in Bethlehem,' I said.

'That's ridiculous!' Herod sneered. 'No genuine king is likely to be born in that backwater.'

He turned to the group of visitors and beckoned them over.

'Tell me again,' he ordered, fixing his gaze on one of them, less well dressed and clearly an interpreter.

'These men say that they have come to see the child born King of the Jews. They saw a star and have followed it and now they want to see him and worship him.'

My heart began pounding. A star! The words of Balaam's prophecy echoed in my head. 'I shall see him, but not now. I shall behold him but not nigh: there shall come a star out of Jacob, and a sceptre shall arise out of Israel . . .'

Could it be that after seven centuries, the prophecy was coming true? This wasn't like all the other times when upstarts and impostors had tried to claim the throne – and lost their heads for their trouble. But none had come so far, and none had mentioned a star.

By now Herod was purple in the face, his hands balled into fists, and his breathing rapid and shallow.

And he was smiling. Which was not a good sign.

He turned to the visitors.

'This is most interesting,' he said. 'Please – go to Bethlehem and search for the child. And when you find him, come back and let me know so that I too may go and worship him.'

My blood turned to ice in my veins. Whatever Herod intended to do when he had located this child, worship certainly didn't feature.

Silence

Hymn

As with gladness men of old

Reading

Matthew 2:16-18

Reflection of the doorkeeper

They never came back, those foreigners. I'd been told to keep a watch out for them and to tell Herod the very instant they appeared.

But they didn't come.

I guess they'd made a mistake about the star and baby thing, and didn't want to show themselves up to be idiots.

Herod seems pretty miffed about it, though. There are rumours that heads will roll. I don't know whose head, but I wouldn't want to be in their shoes right now.

Reflection of a bereaved mother

Gone.

Slaughtered.

Wrenched from my arms, driven through with a sword, his little skull shattered on the stones at my feet.

My son. My child.

And not just mine – all the newborn boys, all the male toddlers in the space of a couple of hours.

Dead.

Gone.

Slaughtered.

And where was God in all that?

Where was the God that rescued us from the hands of the Egyptians? Was it our turn to suffer just as those mothers who were not marked by the blood of a lamb on their doorposts must have suffered?

Why didn't God warn us?

Why weren't we marked with the blood of a lamb this time?

Or doesn't he care?

My neighbour and her man – they left the other day. If they hadn't, their little lad would be where mine is now.

Dead.

Gone.

Slaughtered.

But he's OK. She's the lucky one.

He's alive and my little boy is dead.

I wonder how she'd feel to see her innocent son slaughtered by a bloodthirsty, rampaging mob?

Dead. Gone. Slaughtered. Why, God? Why?

Silence

Reading

Three separate voices (preferably one male, one female and one child) now say the words of 'Till all the jails are empty'. (The text may be found in *Common Ground: A Song Book for All Churches*, edited by John Bell, published by Saint Andrews Press, Edinburgh, 1998.)

Silence

Hymn

Beauty for brokenness

Prayers of intercession

Lord Jesus, take our broken world and mend it; take our breaking hearts and heal them; take our anger and transform it; take our bitterness and sweeten it. Energise us, Lord, to work for justice, to speak for those who have no voice, to feed those whose bodies and minds are empty. Help us to see when a hand held, or a word spoken or a prayer shared can change a life; and, Lord, when it seems that we don't see the changes we hope and pray for, keep us faithful, keep us serving, keep us, Father, close to you. Amen.

Lord, the Magis' faith and insight led them to search for you, despite all the difficulties and challenges of the journey. And when they found you, their lives took a different direction as they obeyed your call. May we, as we move into a new year, be willing and eager to seek you out and be led into a new life, and may the gifts we bring to you be the gifts of devotion, obedience, love and praise. Amen.

(*Here follow intercessory prayers for the congregation, community and wider world.*)

Hymn

Lord, for the years

15

Arrivals and departures

A service for Epiphany

Introduction

Scripture can be frustrating at times; some stories we have in huge detail, others – often ones that challenge and fascinate us – appear to be skimmed over in just the briefest of sentences. We hear in great detail about the visit of the Magi to the infant Christ; but of the flight into Egypt, of the time spent there waiting to return home, of the reaction of Mary and Joseph's friends, family and business associates, there is hardly a word.

Mary and Joseph had not expected to have to escape to Egypt; they had made no preparations for such an upheaval. But when God told them to go, they went. And what of their friends back in Nazareth? Did God send them dreams as well, explaining in detail what was happening? In all probability not. They would have worried and wondered until some travelling merchant or camel herder was able to get a message to them. A merchant or camel herder who probably didn't have even the smallest idea what lay behind the need for this unknown couple to do a runner to a neighbouring country. And probably didn't care.

And then, just weeks later, came an event that would have sent a chill of terror through the hearts of everyone who heard about it. Would anyone have made the connection between the flight of Mary and Joseph and the horrific massacre of all the boys under two years old in the city of Bethlehem?

Would they? Would we?

Hymn

Brightest and best

Reflection of Mary

I had been looking forward so much to seeing all of Joseph's relatives again, to showing Jesus off to them. He had grown into a stocky, happy sixteen-month-old and had just mastered the art of walking without falling over too often, when Joseph, who had never missed celebrating the Passover in Jerusalem, decided we would all go together and visit his family on the way home. The previous year I had stayed behind in Nazareth; Jesus had been fretful and the weather was unseasonably wet and cold – and to be honest I was still a very new and anxious mum and didn't want to expose my baby to a long and tedious journey.

But by the following year life seemed to be settling back into the old familiar pattern; even the sharp-tongued gossips in the village had grown bored of making snide comments about Joseph marrying a fallen woman. Joseph's business was doing well – we weren't rich by any means but we could pay our way and put bread on the table and our goats were producing milk. Life was good and we were in high spirits by the time we arrived at Joseph's family home.

We had a lovely couple of days – it was only meant to be a fleeting visit, as Joseph had work to do in Nazareth and couldn't afford to be away for long. But sometimes, even the best plans go awry – as they did for us, the night before we were due to leave for home.

Taizé chant

In the Lord I'll be ever thankful

or

Hymn

God moves in a mysterious way

Reading

Matthew 2:1-12

Reflection of Joseph

To be honest, I wasn't in the best frame of mind when I opened the door. It was late, I was tired and Mary and I had just settled down for the night. For a moment I was tempted to ignore the knocking, but Mary was quick to point out that it might be one of the neighbours in some kind of need, and since I knew my cousin wouldn't hear it – he had grown deaf in his old age and, besides, he liked to sleep up on the roof in the warmer weather – I scrambled to my feet and went to the door before the commotion could wake Jesus. As I fiddled with the latch, I heard voices outside – and hesitated. These were no neighbours; the language they were speaking was unknown to me and for a moment, I wondered if it was a posse of Roman soldiers come to extort yet another tax from us on some trumped-up charge. But as the knocking began again, I knew I had no choice but to open the door.

Carol

Three Kings from Persian lands afar *or* We three kings of Orient are

Reflection of Melchior

Odd, isn't it, how human beings react to strange situations? I mean, take us three – we'd travelled goodness knows how many miles for months on end, we'd put up with scorching heat, freezing nights, sandstorms that appeared from nowhere and camels going lame at the wrong moment and we'd never had a cross word. Well, almost never – there was the time when Balthazar insisted that we had taken a wrong path and sulked for a couple of hours, but nothing worse than that.

Even when we'd reached the court of King Herod and found out that they hadn't a clue what we were talking about when we spoke of the new King, we kept our cool while they muttered and perused old manuscripts and offered us food that was certainly not to our taste. When they decided that we were in the wrong place, and that the child would be born in Bethlehem – even then we were stoical about the wasted days and set off once more.

And after all that, there we were outside a fairly rundown house in a back street of Bethlehem arguing about what we should do next. To me it was pretty obvious – knock on the door and find the baby we had come all this way to see. End of. But Balthazar said that was ridiculous; that we'd obviously got some of the readings wrong because, yes, the star appeared to be over this house but no way would a future king be living in a place like that. And then Caspar butted in and said that perhaps our perspective was wrong and the star was only appearing to be over this house and was actually in line with another, more opulent residence in another street. In the end, I said there was only one way to find out, so I thumped on the door as hard as I could and prayed that I wasn't going to be made to look an idiot.

Reading

Psalm 72:10, 11, 15

Hymn

O worship the Lord in the beauty of holiness *or* From the eastern mountains *or* Hail to the Lord's anointed

Reflection of Mary

When Joseph opened the door, I thought I must be dreaming. The man standing on the threshold was like no one I had ever seen before. He was tall, dark-skinned and his clothes, although covered with dust and grime, were of rich material, such as people where we lived would never have seen, never mind worn. There were two other men behind him, muttering at one another in low, guttural tones. They were clearly foreigners: I couldn't understand a word they were saying.

For a moment or two the leader – I thought of him that way because he instantly took charge – gabbled away to Joseph. After a moment I realised that he was trying to speak Hebrew – very badly.

'The baby?' I heard Joseph gasp. He turned to me.

'They want to see Jesus,' he said, and the look on his face was one of bewilderment mixed with pride. 'Should we let them?'

At that moment, Jesus, clearly fascinated by what was going on, waved his arms in the air and chuckled.

'Yes!' The man's face lit up and he bowed respectfully to Joseph.

Suddenly I knew it was all right. I didn't have a clue how they knew about Jesus but I felt in my heart that they came in peace. I nodded to Joseph and he waved them in.

To my surprise, they knelt down and gazed at Jesus, who bounced up and down on my lap, happy as usual to be the centre of attention. Then Melchior produced a bag and took out three boxes, richly encrusted with jewels. I actually pinched my arm, just to check I wasn't dreaming. One box contained gold, another frankincense and the third myrrh. The sort of things we could never afford brought by strangers for our baby. It seemed wonderful – and puzzling.

We both thanked them effusively and then Joseph asked the question that had been bothering me.

'How did you find us?'

Melchior laughed and began speaking so fast that Joseph had to hold up his hand to slow him down.

'He says they followed a new star,' Joseph said, his face puckering in a frown. 'He says it stopped here. Over this house. He says they've spent a lifetime waiting for this to happen.'

And then I understood.

Reading

Numbers 24:17a

Hymn

You are the King of Glory (*Hosanna to the Son of David*) *or* What child is this

Reflection of Joseph

It was just as the three men were taking their leave that I heard one of them say the dreaded word: 'Herod.'

My heart raced. If these guys were anything to do with Herod, then, despite appearances, they were bad news. I turned to Melchior and asked him outright what they were talking about. He stumbled over his words and at first I thought he was trying to avoid my question but then I realised that he was struggling to explain with his limited knowledge of Hebrew.

'We are going home,' he said. 'Herod is not good. We will not see him.'

That was good enough for me. I waved them off with more effusive thanks, and went back to bed.

Reading

Matthew 2:13-15

Reflection of Mary

At first, I thought Joseph was having a nightmare. He was kneeling beside me, shaking me frantically and shouting to me to wake up and start packing. I tried to calm him, to remind him that we weren't due to leave for Nazareth until the following day and there would be time to pack in the morning, but he ignored my protests, jumping to his feet and beginning to assemble our belongings into a pile in the corner of the room.

'I have had a dream,' he said. 'An angel of God spoke to me.'

The look in his eyes brooked no argument.

'Go on,' I said, and even before I heard his reply fear gripped my heart.

'Herod plans to kill Jesus.'

It was as if someone had poured ice-cold water through my veins. Instinctively I reached out to Jesus and drew him to me.

'We have to leave at once – Herod is going to mount a search and he won't rest till he's found Jesus. We're going to Egypt.'

I stared at him in disbelief. The Egyptian border was at least three days' journey away and what would we do when we got there? What about our family? Joseph's work? Before I could voice all these thoughts, Joseph drew me to him.

'We have to go,' he said. 'When God speaks we must obey.'

And so it was that we left Bethlehem, not on the road that led home to Nazareth, but along a strange route we had never travelled before. As we turned our back on all that was familiar, I raised my eyes to the star, still shining brightly as the sky lightened in the east. And I prayed that God would go with us and keep us strong, that he would keep us safe so that we could keep his Son safe. And that he would keep safe all those we loved and were leaving behind.

Silence

Prayer

Father God, when we think of Mary, Joseph and the infant Jesus as refugees, displaced persons, forced to seek safety in a country that had at times been outwardly hostile to Israel – it's all at such odds with the tasteful images on our Christmas cards. Uprooted, heading into the unknown, and with no idea how long it would be before they could return, they must have been worried sick, wondering perhaps why you couldn't simply have softened the heart of Herod rather than force them to face yet another challenge. As we think of their journey, so we pray, Lord, for all those who, for whatever reason, are forced to leave their homes – whether through civil war, natural disaster or famine; those who walk for days to find food or medical help, and those who return home to find that their home is no more. And we give thanks for those at the end of the journey who welcome, nurture and nourish the weary while they wait for safer times to return. Amen.

Hymn

Father, I place into your hands

Reading

Matthew 2:16-18

Reflection of a grieving mother of Bethlehem

He's gone. They killed him. My precious little boy, my life, my reason to be – wrenched from my arms, his skull smashed on the stony ground and his lifeless little body kicked out of the way by that brute of a soldier. Why? Why? Oh Lord my God, why? How could you let this happen to me – to all of us? All night the air has been filled with the sounds of wailing – Rebekkah, Miriam, Leah, Naomi, Ruth, Sarai – we have all lost our boys. The air is filled with the stench of blood – the blood of innocent babies shed for what? Some say King Herod is searching for a special child, a child who will threaten his throne – so how come they took our kids? What do we know of thrones and kings and palaces? Why? Why? Oh Lord my God, why? Lord my God, where are you now? Do you care? Did you ever care? Why God did you let this happen? Why my child? What have I ever done to you?

Silence

Prayer

(*Congregational response is in bold type.*)

We bring to you, Lord, those cast down in the pit of grief.

Lord, in your mercy, shine in their darkness.

We bring to you, Lord, those who see no way out of their pain.

Lord, in your mercy, shine in their darkness.

We bring to you, Lord, those who struggle with the guilt of past actions.

Lord, in your mercy, shine in their darkness.

We bring to you, Lord, our confusion as we witness the wrongs of this world, and wonder why. O Lord, why?

Lord, in your mercy, shine in our darkness.

Hymn

There is a hope *or* Beauty for brokenness *or* Hear me, dear Lord

Reflection of Mary

It could have been him. Jesus. What if we hadn't listened? What if we'd put off leaving for Egypt? When we crossed the Wadi El Arish, and entered Egyptian territory, safe from Herod's jurisdiction, Joseph said we could at last relax. But I couldn't; I was so homesick, so worried about my friends and family, so – well, yes – so puzzled as to why God couldn't have just got rid of Herod and saved us all this difficulty. People were kind, that I can't deny – the little Jewish community in Gezer took us to their hearts and Joseph found work; as time passed he got a message to his brother Cleopas asking him to take care of the business. And every night I prayed to God that he would take us safely home again.

And then we heard.

Rumours, at first, from travellers. Then more definite confirmation – from men whose eyes were hollow with grief, who told stories of the massacre of babies, of streets running with blood, of women ripping their clothes from their backs and hurling themselves against rocks in an attempt to assuage their grief. The stories kept coming – the family next door to Joseph's cousin had lost their twin boys; a woman in the neighbouring street saw the baby she had waited 12 years to conceive run through with a spear.

And then we knew. God had saved us – had saved his Son – from this terrible end. And the words of Simeon, the old prophet who had spoken to me at the Temple at the time of Jesus' presentation, came echoing back to me.

'And a sword will pierce your heart also.'

It could have been me. I could have been grieving the loss of my precious son. But God in his wisdom and grace and mercy had saved him. I prayed I would never have to face what those mothers of Bethlehem were facing.

But deep down, I knew this was only the beginning. This time, all was well. This time. But one day . . .

Hymn

Lord, for the years

Blessing and dismissal

Also by Rosie Rushton

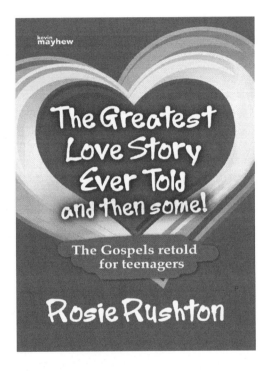

**The Greatest Love Story
Ever Told and then some!**

Paperback 1501285
Hardback 1501286

www.kevinmayhew.com